Walking the Roman Roads of Cumbria

Walking the Roman Roads of Cumbria

James Southworth

ROBERT HALE · LONDON

First published in Great Britain 1985

ISBN 0 7090 2288 3

Robert Hale Limited
Clerkenwell House
Clerkenwell Green
London EC1R 0HT

British Library Cataloguing in Publication Data

Southworth, James
Walking the Roman roads of Cumbria.
1. Roads, Roman—England—Cumbria—
Guide-books 2. Cumbria—Description and travel—Guide-books
I. Title
914.27'8'04858 DG28.5

ISBN 0-7090-2288-3

To my wife for her forebearance,
understanding and practical help

Photoset in North Wales by
Derek Doyle & Associates, Mold, Clwyd
Printed in Great Britain by
Dotesios (Printers) Ltd, Bradford-on-Avon, Wiltshire
Bound by WBC Bookbinders Limited

CONTENTS

LIST OF ILLUSTRATIONS

Photographs by the author

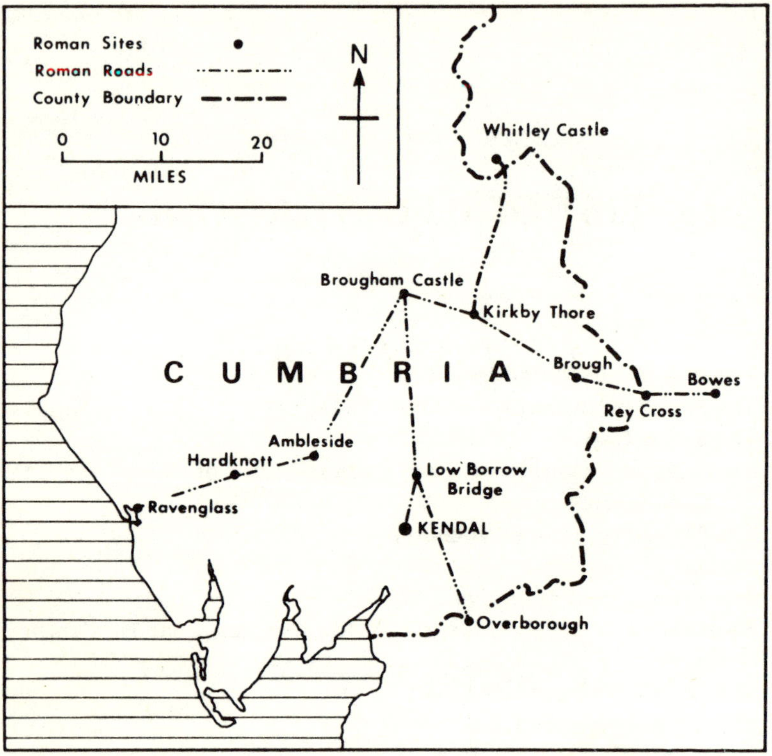

LEGEND

Roman route	Gate
Walker s & route Roman	Cattlegrid
Diversion	Stile
Railway	SP Sign post
Track	Miles from start
Stone wall	Trees: broad leaf
Hedgerow	Trees: coniferous
Fence	Crags
500 Feet above sea level	Buildings
Roman agger	Church

INTRODUCTION

This book has been written for the reader and walker with an interest in and understanding of the countryside and its heritage in general, and for those who have a particular interest in the period of the Roman occupation of these islands. I do not claim the book to be a serious archaeological study but simply the thoughts and observations of a dedicated amateur, and the opinions expressed, although my own, except where otherwise stated, are based on considerable research and backed by extensive fieldwork and on-site study.

The book is fundamentally a walker's guide, designed for the type of walker who likes to mix the sheer pleasure of walking with a knowledge and awareness of the countryside around him.

The work involved in the planning and compiling of the guide has spanned all seasons of the year and many miles of travel. Every Roman foot of the way has been walked by the author at least twice, many sections three or four times. Every moment and mile have been sheer poetry. If I can share some of this pleasure with others of similar sentiment, it can only increase the feeling of achievement which this project has given me.

With one exception, each chapter of the book covers an approximate seventeen- to twenty-mile stretch along the various routes, which follows the Roman army's marching day of twenty miles, the Roman mile being slightly shorter than our own. (See note 1.)

The twenty-mile stretch is also convenient for our purpose because of the Roman practice of wherever possible building forts one day's marching distance apart. I do not expect every reader to try to emulate the marching prowess of the legions, and in most cases the routes can be split up into more manageable sections. The practical aspects of following the routes and the sometimes necessary diversions are covered by the hand-drawn maps which are approximately to scale and as accurate as possible, but in addition I have attempted to convey to the reader something of the flavour of the countryside through which the routes pass and the places of interest both past and present.

My interest in Roman roads stems from many years of fell-wandering around the northern hills, and I became intrigued by the fragments of old trackways encountered, marked on the Ordnance Survey maps as Roman road or course of Roman road. Who were these road-builders and why did they choose to construct their routes across these even today remote fells? Where were they going and why? Thus was my imagination caught.

Part of the answer to these questions was to be found in the monumental work of Ivan Margary, whose authoritative account of the British Roman road system was published in 1955–7. I.D. Margary was a wealthy Sussex landowner whose interest in Roman roads stems from his discovery in 1929 of an unrecorded Roman road crossing his property, an interest he maintained until his death in 1976. Basing his research on an earlier work by a civil engineer named Thomas Codrington, he first covered the Roman roads of Sussex, Surrey and parts of Kent before embarking on the nearly impossible task of plotting the whole Roman road system of Britain. Under the auspices of the Council of British Archaeology he travelled over 20,000 miles, much of it in his immaculate vintage Austin car. He devised a road numbering system, single figures for important routes, double for secondary roads and three figures for minor ones. Such was the quality of his work that he became the leading authority and the doyen of Roman road studies. The highest accolade a discoverer of a Roman road could receive was to have his road allocated a Margary Roman road number and this was only done after a visit to the site by the master himself. A later, one-volume edition, of his book was published in 1967 and although now out of print a copy can usually be found in the reference section of most libraries.

It is due to Margary's work that I was able to link those fragments of track together and became inspired to produce a detailed practical guide to those routes which have a scenic as well as a historical interest to walker and reader alike. Fortunately many of the northern routes pass through wild marginal land which has remained untouched through the centuries, and consequently considerable remains can be seen and the original alignments followed.

The arterial Roman road system in the North of England, of which the Cumbrian section is an integral part, is comparatively simple, built mainly by the conquering legions of Julius Agricola during his campaign against the Brigantes in the years AD 79–80, and with additional roads constructed during the reign of the Emperor Hadrian some forty years later. We are told by the Roman historian Tacitus that Agricola split his forces into two columns. The Ninth Legion from its fortress at York marched north along the eastern slopes of the Pennines; the second column, led by the Twentieth Legion and under the command of Agricola himself, headed up the western side. These two main campaign routes were then linked, in the south through the Aire Gap and in the north through the Stainmore Gap. Thus the region was contained into a neat Roman package with forts strategically placed along its borders. The advance continued northwards, establishing forts and connecting roads along the way until at the end of the first year's campaign the Tyne-Solway isthmus was reached.

The area covered by this book centres on the site of the Roman fort of Brocavum, situated near the confluence of the Rivers Eamont and Lowther and under the shadow of the later medieval castle of Brougham (locally pronounced 'Brawm'). The site has been strategically important since it was established by Agricola to protect the river-crossing and was an early focus of Roman roads in the region as well as a meeting point of the two main campaign routes. It is also most convenient for our purpose, situated as it is 1½ miles south-east of the attractive old county town of Penrith, now a bustling tourist centre and boasting a wide variety of accommodation to suit all tastes and with easy access for road and rail travellers.

Students of Roman Britain will be well aware that this book does not cover all the Roman roads of Cumbria, as there are several radiating to and from Carlisle as well as the coastal route connecting the forts and fortlets of the sea-coast extension of Hadrian's Wall. These have yet to be walked and may well be the subject of a further book. What I have done is pick out those roads with which I am familiar and which have a particular scenic value and historical interest, and which also make for pleasurable walking.

So many of these ancient and strategic routes have been buried under tons of concrete as modern progress obliterates the past glories of our Roman heritage. Since commencing this book such a fate overtook one of the routes planned, (Margary's route 75) but because it still fulfils two of the required criteria – being of particular historical interest and of scenic value – I have included it in the last chapter: not as a walker's route but as one which can still be enjoyed for the places of interest along it.

To understand fully the reasons behind the campaigns of Agricola, and in fact the Roman presence at all, we have to go back forty years earlier. Most of us were taught at school that Julius Caeser first landed in Britain in the year 55 BC, but it is not generally appreciated that it was not until nearly one hundred years later, in the spring of AD 43, during the reign of the Emperor Claudius, that a Roman army of four legions with supporting auxiliary troops, amounting in all to about forty thousand men, began what was to be the eventual conquest of Britain. Two of these four legions, the Ninth and the Twentieth, were to remain in Britain for a great number of years and indeed were to play a leading part in the shaping of northern Britain. (See note 2.)

From these early days of the Roman presence until the appointment of Petillius Cerialis as Governor in AD 71, the neutral Brigantian kingdom protected the northern flank of the province. It stretched from sea to sea on an approximate line between the Mersey and the Humber, blocking the entire north, and made unnecessary the deployment of any large Roman force in the area. But in AD 71 the kingdom ruled by Queen Cartimandua was weakened by dynastic strife and became unstable. The Queen divorced her husband, Venutius, who had assumed the leadership of a strong anti-Roman element amongst the Brigantes and was already looking north for allies in the Scottish tribes, and then she appealed for Roman aid when Venutius declared open war against her. A force of auxiliary infantry and cavalry was dispatched but succeeded only in rescuing the Queen and was unable to defeat Venutius and restore the kingdom.

Thus when Cerialis took over his office of Governor, a now actively hostile power faced and threatened the northern frontier of the province. The breakdown of the Brigantian alliance had far-reaching consequences: Rome had no alternative but to attempt the complete subjection of the whole island. Once it was subdued, the large, costly garrison of Britain could be reduced. But the resistant character of the hill people, strengthened and embittered by refugees from the southern tribes, proved in the end to be unrelentingly hostile, and from this time on Rome was committed to maintain large military forces in Britain which she could ill afford.

In fact, for most of the long years of Roman occupation of Britain, the island was to be the most heavily garrisoned province of the Empire, a remarkable fact when one considers the size of Britain compared with the very much larger and more populated areas of the Rhine and the Danube. It also says much for the value that Rome placed on the province through the centuries, tying down substantial forces in its defence even when under great pressure along its land frontiers much nearer home.

Of Cerialis's campaign against the Brigantes very little is

known in detail. Tacitus tells us merely that after a number of battles most of the country was overrun and conquered. The difficulty of tracing the footsteps of Cerialis is due to his neglect of fort-building. Apart from the new fortress at York which he built for the Ninth Legion, the only other bases which could suggest anything pre-Agricolan are at Carlisle in Cumbria and possibly Lancaster further south. Further evidence of this campaign can be seen at the summit of Stainmore Pass, where the outlines of a twenty-acre marching camp are still visible (see note 3), with traces of two other, similar camps spaced a day's march apart on a line pointing towards Carlisle.

Venutius is reputed to have made his last stand at Stanwick, a massive hill fort on a strategic position near what is now known as Scotch Corner. The hill fort with its perimeter dikes had been enlarged several times in the preceding years, and Cerialis's rapid advance found some of the latest work still unfinished. The fort, built to contain and defend a large number of tribesmen and their herds, was considered by the Britons to be the most advanced of its kind but was no match for a legionary attack; its very size made it almost impossible to defend.

Nothing more is heard of Venutius, so we can assume that he died in the battle, Early in AD 74 Cerialis was recalled to Rome, leaving the Brigantes scattered and leaderless, but no steps were taken to police the conquered territory or to incorporate it formally into the province.

The next stage of our story begins in AD 78 with the return of Gnaeus Julius Agricola as Governor of Britain. Agricola was no stranger to Britain or indeed to the north, having first served as a military tribune under the Governor Paulinus in AD 60 and taken part in the offensive against the Druids of Anglesey and later played a major part as Legate i.e. Commander of the Twentieth Legion under Cerialis during his campaigns.

On arrival, Agricola immediately reviewed the situation: the north was still hostile, and the tribes were gathering once more; an uprising in Wales had annihilated a Roman garrison there; the army was idle and demoralized. His first act was to mount a successful punitive expedition against the rebelling Ordovices of North Wales, which also restored the morale of his troops. He then turned his attention towards the north, and in AD 79 the great advance began.

From this campaign resulted many of the roads covered by the guide, and as the walker strides out across the fells in the footsteps of Agricola's legions, he or she will not be able to help but wonder at the sheer magnitude of the task undertaken and the skill of these military road-builders of nearly two thousand years ago.

Much has been written on the subject of Roman roads, showing methods of surveying and construction details, and I have no wish to duplicate too much of this information. But for the benefit of those of my readers who are unfamiliar with the subject, I think that it is important to cover briefly a few main points so that the routes can be fully appreciated.

The most common misconception regarding Roman roads is that all are straight. Of course the Roman engineers were well aware that the shortest distance between two points was a straight line, and there are many fine examples of this, particularly across the flat plains, but in hilly country the reverse is often true. A winding course which follows the lie of the land was often the most convenient and quickest way to surmount a natural obstacle. The line of the road is called the alignment and was usually determined from a high position on the terrain, referred to as the sighting point. The alignment was placed to avoid major difficulties, but where local obstacles were encountered, such as a river valley, the road would be turned along the hillside on a well-graded terraceway to resume the original alignment when the obstacle was passed. On a steep hillside, perhaps descending to a river-crossing, a series of zigzag terraces would be cut. It is noteworthy that Roman roads nearly always make important turns upon high ground from which the new sighting can be made.

For the most part Roman roads were laid upon a well-constructed embankment to provide a well-drained base for the road; the material for this embankment, called an agger, was excavated from a ditch along one or, more commonly, both sides of the chosen route. The size of the agger varied greatly in both height and width depending on the importance of the route, up to five feet high and fifty feet wide on some of the major routes, but only one foot or less high and down to twelve feet wide on others.

Upon this agger was laid the road proper, first a foundation of large stones and then successive layers of well-rammed gravels, flints and other suitable local materials. As the road advanced across the changing countryside, so would the surface nature in accordance with the material available.

Paved surfaces were very rarely constructed in this country, the road over Blackstone Edge near Manchester being a rare example of this type. On most roads in this country the larger stones were used for the foundations, or in some cases as edging stones to hold firm the surface material. River-crossings were usually by means of a paved ford, and where bridges were necessary they would be of a wooden construction.

As already stated, the pattern of the Roman roads of this part of the Northern Province, which we now know as Cumbria, was set by the Agricolan campaign in the first place, but the events that followed (which resulted in the building of a physical barrier, Hadrian's Wall, to separate the Brigantes from the tribes of southern Scotland) had a lasting effect on the area. As the fortunes of the Empire ebbed and flowed, so did the degree of military control, but right through to the final withdrawal of the last of the legions in the fourth century the whole of the Northern Province was to remain a military zone.

Because of the unsettled nature of the area, the majority of the roads built were of a military nature, connecting forts or other military establishments of a supporting role. Thus the area differed from that in the more southerly parts of the province, where the settled nature and higher degree of Romanization of the population created trade and commerce, which in turn led to the construction of many more roads under the control of the civil authorities. In fact by the third century

Britain was divided into two separate provinces and even later, in the fourth century, into five.

For those interested, the methods used in compiling the guide were in several stages. First, the route chosen was surveyed using the standard Ordnance Survey map of Roman Britain together with Margary's *Guide to the Roman Roads of Britain*. I then took a closer look at the route, using the 1:25,000 scaled maps, $2\frac{1}{2}$ inches to 1 mile, which show details such as field boundaries and public footpaths. My next and most important step was to walk the route, seeking out practical diversions where necessary and making on-site observations and detailed drawings of the actual walker's guide. Only essential details could be included, but even so the guides are simple to follow. The symbols indicating dry-stone walls, hedges etc are drawn to give a general impression of the route, except where it becomes vital to route-finding, and this will be shown in the appropriate text. A number within a circle shows the mileage from the start of each individual route, and this distance on the maps may vary slightly, depending on the amount of detail.

It is common practice for maps to be drawn with north to the top, but as this guide, radiating as it does from a fixed central base, heads for different points of the compass, the result would be somewhat confusing. I have therefore deviated from the normal practice and have so drawn the maps that the route is followed by the reader from the bottom of the page to the top, with a compass heading to indicate the direction. As each individual route follows an overall straight alignment between two Roman sites, this practice should not create any problems for the walker following the guide.

You will note that at the beginning of each chapter I recommend that the appropriate Ordnance Survey maps should be also carried. This is not essential for the actual following of the route but simply adds to the enjoyment of the walk and heightens the appreciation of the Roman achievement.

Where the Roman route crosses cultivated or marginal land on other than established foot or bridle-paths, the author has made every effort to seek out the nearest right of way to enable the walker to follow as closely as possible the original alignment. There are occasions when such pathways, through lack of use, are not well defined or even sign-posted and it is the individual walker's responsibility to check such rights of way *or* in case of doubt seek permission before proceeding. It has been the author's experience over many years that even if no right of way exists permission is very rarely refused if the approach is made with courtesy and a reasonable explanation given. Most country people are rightly proud of their own piece of ancient history and are generous with their information and help.

If a public right of way passes through farm property, I always check and ask permission and I strongly advise the followers of my guide to do the same. Only by establishing good relations at a personal level can the rights of both parties be fostered and protected and the benefits shared by all. So much ill feeling has been, in my opinion, created by certain ramblers arrogantly demanding their rights irrespective of the feelings of farmers and possibly a particular circumstance prevailing at the time. All so often a simple polite and cheerful 'good day to you' followed by 'is it all right if ...' is all that is required to foster a feeling of good will.

May I make one further plea to potential walkers of the guide, *please* no large parties. Nothing I am sure, is more disturbing to the livestock and to the wild life on the moors than a long line of brightly cagoule-clad, chattering ramblers. Only by listening to the silence of the fells and drinking in the atmosphere of these ancient routes can the imagination take us back to the days when the legions of Rome tramped the very ground beneath our feet.

Several of the routes described can be safely walked in all seasons of the year under almost all conditions, others which take the traveller above the 1,000 ft contour line require more care, both in the choice of season and of the clothing worn. Even a hot summer's day can have its hazards of heat stroke and dehydration. Advice as to the best time and conditions of the individual routes can be found at the beginning of each chapter together with other relevant information. Chapters 1 and 6 involve the crossing of grouse moors and should be avoided for several weeks from the 12 of August onwards. The author would expect all walkers to respect the usual countryside code of conduct regarding litter, wild flowers and shutting of gates etc.

CHAPTER 1

Brougham Castle (Brocavum) to Low Borrow Bridge (Alone). Margary's route 7c. 19 miles.

About the road

This is perhaps one of the most historically important of the routes described in this book. It forms part of the great western campaign route of Agricola, laid down in AD 79. The alignment of the route was most likely surveyed and established by the engineers of the Twentieth Legion, which led the advance northwards from the legionary fortress of Derva at Chester. As the legions advanced and pacified the country, forts were constructed and connecting roads built to facilitate communications and supplies. The forts of Brocavum and Alone are but two of this chain of fortifications. The route continued northwards to what was later to become Hadrian's Wall and also to the important administrative centre at Carlisle, and would have been much used right throughout the whole period of the Roman occupation. When one considers that, during the second century and beyond, the wall forts alone were manned by something in the region of 9,500 men, one can imagine the vast quantity of supplies and equipment moving along these main routes. Based on records and research, it has been estimated that, for a period in the second century, northern England as a whole was held by a total of 26,000 troops.

The first half of the route described in this chapter is along quiet country lanes which in the most part follow the Roman alignments fairly faithfully in a south-east direction, passing through rich pastures and cultivated woodlands until the small hamlet of Reagill is reached.

Just beyond Reagill we leave the metalled lanes to follow the Roman alignment across the rough fells and grouse moors. Here numerous earthworks, and remains of Iron Age settlements are to be found, including the large Romano-British settlement of Ewe Close, near which the Roman road passes. As the road climbs up the shoulder of Coalpit Hill at about a thousand feet, the highest point on the route, the original alignment can still be detected. A slight turn to the south and the well-defined track drops down the fellside towards the twin highways of the M6 motorway. As we approach the motorway, the twenty-one foot agger can be seen very plainly, with a deep ditch on either side. The last two miles of the route to Low Borrow Bridge have been for the most part obliterated by railway and roadwork constructions, sharing as they do the same route through the Tebay Gap. Our way is by a narrow, often sunken lane which leads down to the Lune Bridge, halfway between Tebay town and Low Borrow Bridge. This last section is an ancient route which for some part has been adopted from its Roman origin.

The route is comparatively easy to follow, and as it does not rise to any great height, no special clothing is required other than a good pair of walking shoes or boots. I prefer the more rigid type of boot for road walking, but everyone to their own choice. The route does suffer from one disadvantage, in so much as the area through which it passes, being off the tourist route, possesses very few places of refreshment. The almost silent hamlets along the route have neither shop nor pub, and a detour to the nearby village at Crosby Ravensworth was, on my last visit, a sad disappointment. The landlord of the Butcher's Arms had taken the day off. I'm sure the Romans fared better.

At either end of the route there is no problem of accommodation. Penrith, is of course, within easy reach of Brougham, and there is alternative good family accommodation available at the Crown Hotel at Eamont, approximately two miles west of Brougham Castle, as described in Chapter 4. At the southern end of the route, both Tebay and Orton, 2½ miles north, can supply most needs.

The finest section of the route is that from Reagill to the motorway crossing, but avoid the grouse season (the Glorious 12 August) at all costs, as then such a journey would be hazardous in the extreme. The Ordnance Survey Map, Landranger Series, sheet 91, should be carried as well as the guide to give an overall picture of the surrounding countryside.

The Route
Map 1

The site of the Roman fort of Brocavum is situated 1½ miles south-east of Penrith. It lies within a stone's-throw of Brougham Castle, which can be reached by a minor road, the B6262, running between the A66 and the A6 (map reference NY5328).

The medieval castle of Brougham is under the protection of the Ministry of the Environment, who charge a small entrance fee. It began as a Norman keep and was extended over the centuries. From the thirteenth century it came under the control of the Clifford family, and it suffered some considerable damage during the civil wars. It was derelict until the advent of Lady Anne Clifford (1590–1676), who devoted her long life and formidable energy to restoring the castles of Cumbria. In addition to Brougham, she repaired all the Clifford castles, including Brough, built on another Roman site, and Appleby, Pendragon and Skipton.

The site of the Roman fort does not come under the control of the Ministry, and consequently there is no sign or notice board to record its existence, which is a great pity. It can best be viewed from the crossroads where the B6262 meets the minor road leading to the castle. The ditch and raised earthworks can clearly be identified, and the site covers an area of approximately 4½ acres, a size sufficient to house a garrison a thousand strong. Serious excavations of the site have never taken place, and what information we have has come from chance finds of pottery, coins and inscriptions.

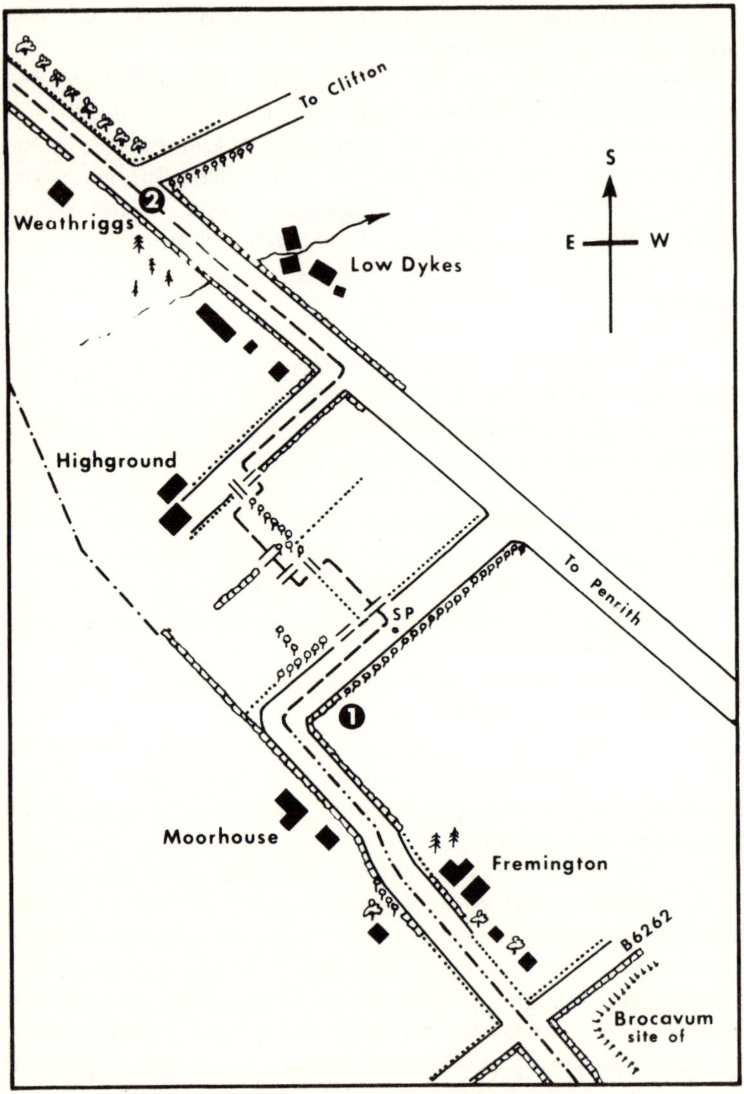

To Clifton
S
E
W
Weathriggs
Low Dykes
Highground
To Penrith
SP
Moorhouse
Fremington
B6262
Brocavum
site of

Map 1

Originally constructed of turf and timber, it was rebuilt of stone in the second century, as were many of Agricola's forts. The occupation of Brocavum continued right through to the fourth century. An altar stone, dated to the third century, records that a unit of auxiliary cavalry (see note 3), named the *Numerus Equitum Stratonicianorum*, was stationed here at one time. The title is probably derived from a city in Asia Minor called Stratonicaea, from which the legion was originally recruited. A further stone was found dedicated to a tribune of the Eighth Legion, which was responsible for building part of Hadrian's Wall.

There is evidence of a fairly large settlement of legionary veterans in the immediate area, similar to the one established outside the fort at Ribchester further south along the same campaign route. These veteran settlements, made up of legionaries who had completed their twenty-five years' service, were encouraged by the Roman authorities by grants of land. They not only provided a trained reserve force but also hastened the spread of urban development, which to the Romans spelled civilization. They were also a source of military-orientated recruits, the sons of the veterans were automatically classed as Roman citizens – although all the inhabitants of the Empire, with the exception of slaves, were, in the second century, during the reign of Caracalla, granted Roman citizenship. There is much to suggest that legions such as the Twentieth, units of which remained on station in Britain for all of three hundred years, had, by the fourth century, become almost exclusively Romano-British.

Leaving the now silent, deserted site of this once bustling centre of military activity, we take the minor road leaving the fort area in a south-easterly direction. The road, which in fact is little more than a lane, maintains a fairly straight and level course for approximately half a mile, passing the farm buildings and imposing house and grounds of Fremington. Where the lane makes an almost ninety-degree turn south-west, the Roman alignment continues on its original course, but unfortunately there is no discernible trace to be seen, and as it crosses private land without public rights of way, it is necessary to make our first diversion from the true route. Continue along the lane, now heading south, until a public highway sign indicates a footpath to the farmstead of Highground, to be seen across the fields to the south-east. This is not a short cut but simply saves some road walking. At the time of writing, the right of way had been blocked by a wire fence (a point I have taken up with the local authority), so I have marked out an alternative route through a series of gates, eventually to gain access to the farm lane between Highground and the old Penrith to Appleby via Bolton road. (This alternative route is not official, and the faint heart would be better perhaps keeping to the lane and turning left at the main road.)

From the entrance to the farm lane, proceed along the main road, which dips to pass a group of buildings known as Low Dykes; note the red sandstone which seems to make up most of the building material of walls etc. The road climbs to pass a small plantation of trees and Wetherigg Pottery. Formerly used for the production of roof tiles and bricks, the pottery now produces a wide variety of household and garden ceramics. The workshop is open to the public, and a selection of craft wares are on sale, together with light refreshments. Now is the time to have that last cup of tea.

Map 2

Immediately beyond the pottery, the road crosses the course of a length of the dismantled old London North Eastern Railway which ran between Penrith and Darlington, and traces can be seen to the right of the road. After passing the turn-off to Lowther, the road levels and runs straight for just over one mile, very much like a Roman road but not so in this case. Our true Roman route, diagonally cutting in from the north-west, crosses the modern road near the junction of the Lowther road, eventually to rejoin us along the edge of Gilshaughlin Wood, two miles ahead.

The mile to our turn-off along the road to Newby is probably the most uninteresting, being a main road. Wide grass verges,

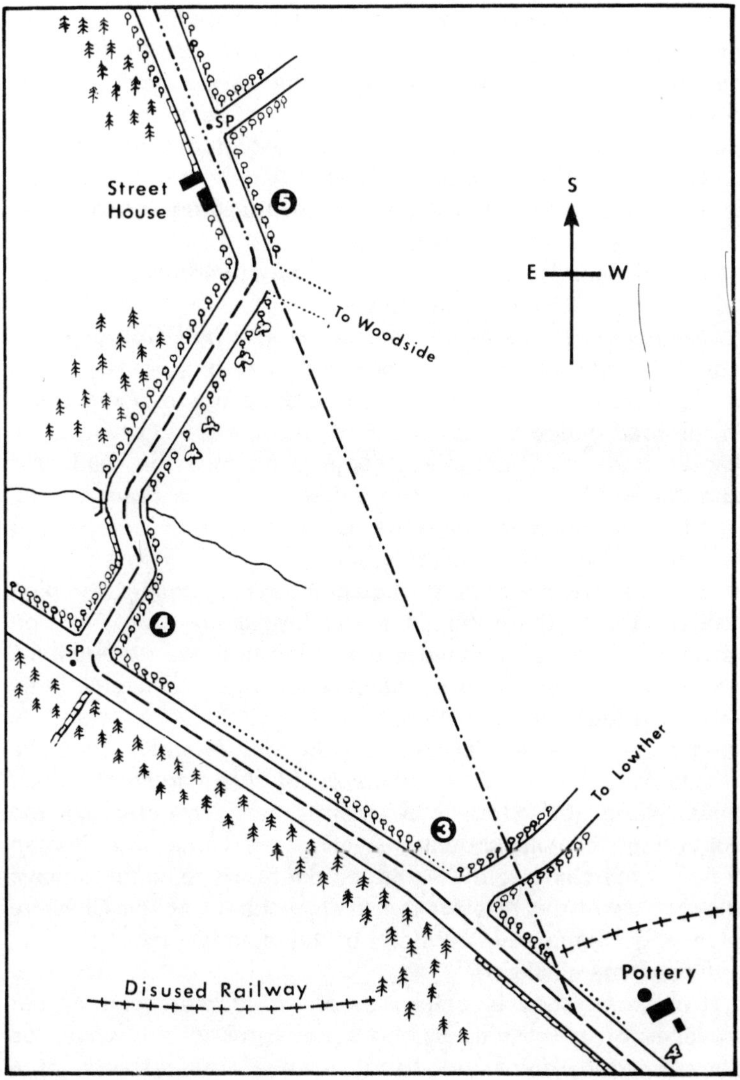
SP
Street House
5
S
E
W
To Woodside
SP
4
To Lowther
3
Pottery
Disused Railway

Map 2

however, make for easy walking as we pass the Ling Plantation of conifers which form part of the Lowther Estate, with the Whinfell Forest rising six hundred feet to the north. To the south, the River Leith winds its gentle way across the lush pastures, an area well known for its pedigree herds of dairy cattle. One of the finest and largest milk depots in the country is situated at Appleby, collecting from the farms of the Eden Valley; it has in the past supplied towns and cities as far away as London, and is now involved in the production of cheese and yoghurt as well as egg-collecting.

A signpost indicates the road to Newby. We drop down to effect the crossing of the young River Leith by Commonholme Bridge before beginning the long, straight climb to where a turn in the road bridge brings us in line with the true Roman route known here as 'The Street'. For a good mile the road runs straight and level, and we can stride out in fine Roman style, passing the farmstead with the name of Street House bearing witness to the road's ancient origins.

Between the plantations of quick-growing conifers, the high mass of the northern Pennines, the largest single area of high ground in England, dominates the scene to the north and east. Along the slopes of Cross Fell, which rises to nearly three thousand feet, runs the Roman road to Whitley Castle and its long haul to the frontier wall. On this day in early spring the slopes were covered by a fine mantle of gleaming snow, whilst here, along the Street, the mantle was reflected by the scatterings of wild snowdrops lining the verge. The Roman traveller marching south would, no doubt, be thankful to leave the rigours of the hills for the milder climate of the Cheshire plain and comparative comforts of the legionary base at Deva, five days' march ahead.

Our view today is quite different from that seen by our traveller of old. Here on the lower ground he would be surrounded by thick woodlands, cleared the distance of a spear's-throw on either side of the road – not the regimented conifers of today but a natural habitat of oak and hazel, the most common in the north, and also elm, birch, beech, ash and alder. The Romans were great users of timber, preferring oak to any other. Massive beams twelve inches square were used on the fort gateways, held together by ten-inch nails. It has been estimated that over eleven thousand acres of timber were felled by the Romans forces to build the forts of northern Britain, but even that amount would hardly thin the British forests. Only on the ground above a thousand feet would the trees thin out and the views which we can appreciate today be visible to our early traveller.

Map 3

After crossing the junction with the minor Appleby to Great Strickland road, our way drops once more to cross Greengill Syke near Syke House and to climb up to the hamlet of Newby. At Newby Head, turn right at the crossroads. Newby Hall, a fine stone building, lies across from the crossroad along the King's Meaburn to Shap road. Our way is by the narrow lane leading off to the left and signposted Sleagill. The banked lane twists and turns between ancient dry-stone walls and hedges, but still maintains an overall south-easterly direction. Margary suggests that the straighter original Roman alignment is slightly to the east of the actual lane, although there is no evidence of this to show.

Crossing Sandwath Bridge and the gill of the same name (*wath* being the old Norse word meaning ford), the lane rises to pass the farmstead of Mill Flat; a further hundred yards and the lane divides. Take the left-hand fork, which after about half a mile reaches the small village of Sleagill.

Map 4

Even Kenneth Smith in his informative book on Cumbrian villages cannot find very much to say about these small, remote hamlets which nestle so quietly, far from the beaten track. There is practically no traffic to disturb the peace of the countryside, and in fact on my last visit I walked the four miles from Street House without meeting a single person, on foot or otherwise.

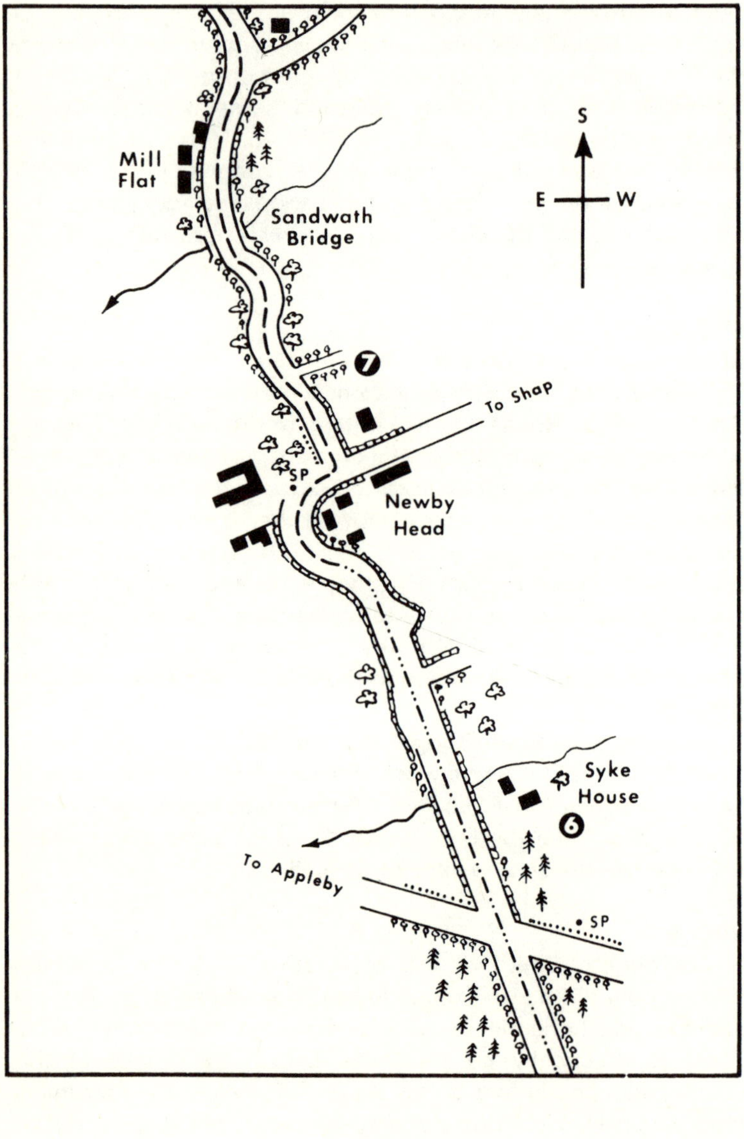
S
E
W
Mill Flat
Sandwath Bridge
7
To Shap
SP
Newby Head
Syke House
6
To Appleby
SP

Map 3

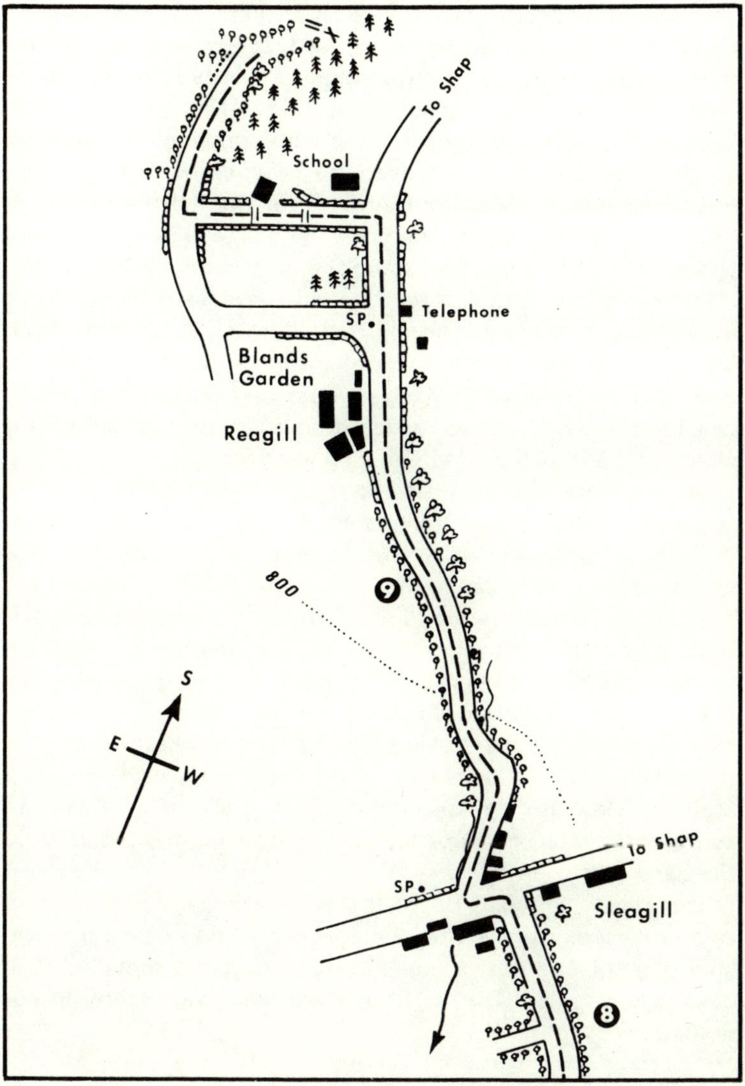
To Shap
School
Telephone
SP.
Blands
Garden
Reagill
800
9
S
E
W
To Shap
SP.
Sleagill
8

Map 4

It would be pretty safe to state that there would have been much more activity going on in the first and second century than there is today, but then we must remember that this route was in those days the equivalent of today's M6 motorway with long trains of pack animals loaded with supplies, new recruits for the legions heading north to the Wall, veterans on release heading south. Troops from all parts of the Empire served in Britain and particularly in the north, so it would not be unusual to see units of bearded Gauls and Syrian archers, who, from the evidence of inscriptions found, could have been stationed at Bravoniacum (Kirkby Thore), and Sarmatian cavalry from Ribchester patrolling the roads of the area. No doubt, with all this activity, road-repair gangs would be constantly at work, causing the usual delays, which goes to show that life hasn't changed that much in nineteen hundred years.

At the T-junction turn left and take the small lane besides a stream on your right, signposted Reagill. Originally written 'Renegil' and sometimes 'Refesgille', the name means 'ravine of the foxes' and, like most names in the area, is of Norse origin. It has one house of interest, that of Thomas Bland the sculptor, who a century ago went about the district setting up monuments to commemorate notable historical events. We shall find an example of his work further along our route. His garden of images lies behind the dry-stone wall opposite the telephone box and bordering the narrow lane signposted to Maulds Meaburn; a peep over the wall will reveal an astonishing array of carved statuary, from heraldic beasts to Grecian urns.

Our way is straight on to the tiny old village school, now sadly disused. Turn left by the school building down a rough lane which leads past a stone cottage to join a metalled lane beyond two gates. Turn right: we are now once more on our Roman alignment.

Map 5

After a short distance the quiet, very attractive lane, with its high hedges and grassy banks, drops down to Reagill Grange.

The fine sixteenth-century hall was built on the site of a monastic grange which was granted to the monks of Shap Abbey during the reign of King John. After the Dissolution it became the property of Lord Wharton and from thence became Lowther land, now busy as a mixed farm. Do not be misdirected by the bridlepath sign to Maulds Meaburn: our way is through the farm, passing the hall on your left, to a gate and onto a broad farm track with a plantation of conifers on your right. Do not hesitate to ask for directions if confused; you will find the occupiers of the hall most helpful.

Look out for the rabbits which scamper back into the trees as you make a quiet approach. Rabbits, some say, were brought here by the Romans, and it is quite true that they were probably the first importers of rabbits into Britain from Spain – rabbit being considered a delicacy. There is no evidence, however, to show that the present rabbit population is descended from Roman stock; it is more likely to have been introduced in the reigns of the Plantagenet kings Henry II and Richard I, who may possibly have brought them back to England on their return through Europe from the Crusades.

As we leave the plantation behind and enter open country, a small stream crosses the path through a culvert: this is Low Wood Beck. Before crossing, leave the path and cross the open land to your right, heading uphill towards the corner of a small wood, crossing the beck on your way. Where the fence meets the wood, a frail stile gives you access to the field beyond: beware of the barbed wire. The public footpath, for such it is, continues uphill, following the boundary of the wood and lying very faint on the ground. What is more important is that this is the true Roman route. As we climb the hill, the evidence of the existence of the agger becomes more clear, with some of the foundation stones as laid by the Roman legionaries nineteen hundred years ago exposed. On reaching the top of the hill, at eight hundred feet, we have a good view of the long range of the Pennines to the north and east and the rich Eden Valley below. The green pastures around us are scattered with numerous sheep and their lambs in early spring, the peace and quiet only occasionally disturbed by the training planes of the Royal Air Force as they practise low-level flying down the valley, the hills high above them.

After passing through a series of gates, we join a farm lane which leads to and through the farm settlement of Wickerslacks, a clear indication that we are now on the Roman road known here as Wicker Street. Passing through the extensive and seemingly expanding settlement (a new barn was being constructed on my last visit), we turn right after passing a beautiful old stone barn along a broad farm track. Follow the dry-stone wall as it turns left, passing through a gate to follow a stony track by an open fell. The way is perfectly clear as we follow this track, eventually to pass a further plantation of young conifers to reach the Crosby Ravencroft to Shap road at Haberwain.

According to the Ordnance map there is a public footpath leading from the farm at Haberwain through the fields to our next point at Haber, but the confusion of farm buildings and the lack of a direction sign make it difficult to find. A better plan is to head up the road towards Shap, passing on your way a grove of very tall trees of elm and giant redwood. Just before the road turns right, a gate gives access to open grasslands, and the way, a broad farm track, is indicated by a footpath sign. The track crosses the open field to pass through two gates by the ruined buildings of High Haber. This is a high point on the route at a thousand feet and was most probably used by the Roman surveyors as a sighting point for plotting the road.

As the track begins to drop down to the farm in the dale below, our route ahead is clearly revealed for many miles. Immediately across the dale, spread out before us, is the Romano-British settlement of Ewe Close, more impressive at this distance than when passing through it. This almost aerial view gives a good idea of the extent of the site, which covers four acres.

Beyond the ancient settlement lies the mixed terrain of Crosby Ravensworth Fell, with its rough pastures and grouse moors of heather and bracken, a rich and colourful sight in late

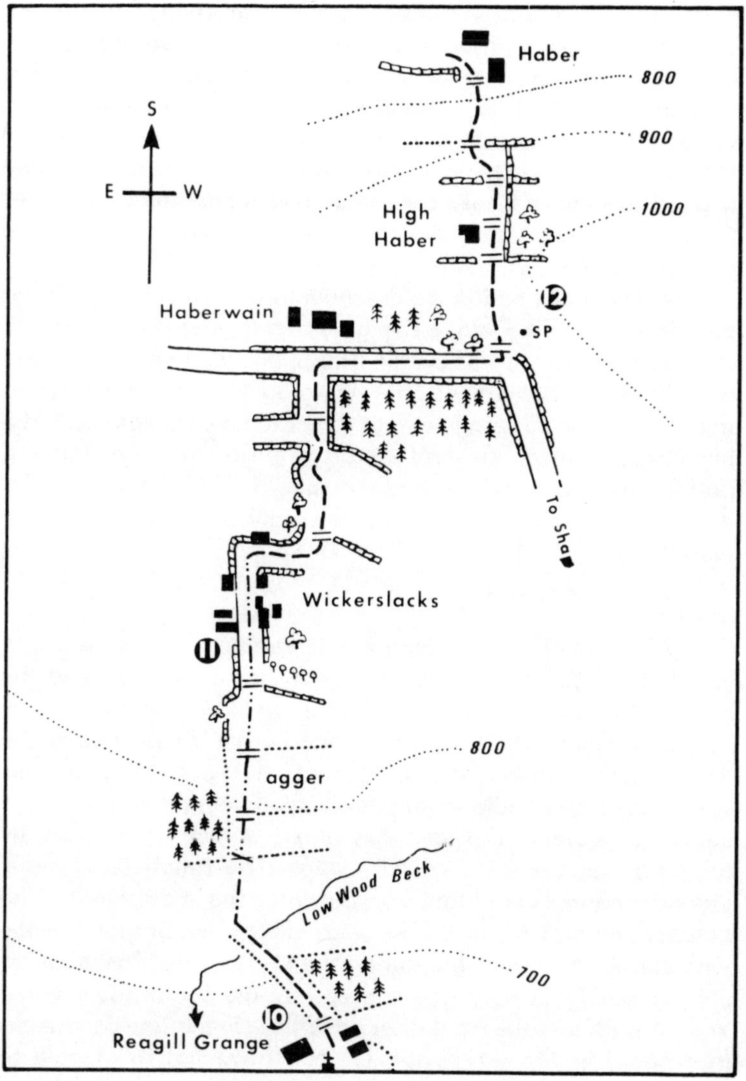
Haber
800
S
900
E
W
High
Haber
1000
12
Haberwain
SP
To Shap
Wickerslacks
11
800
agger
Low Wood Beck
700
10
Reagill Grange

Map 5

summer and autumn. From a point near Haber, the route, looking south, turns more south-west, and a green broad track can be seen, for a short way, climbing towards the rising ground of Coalpit Hill. This is the Roman road and our way to come. In the distance can be seen the bare peaks of the Whinfell ridge and the Howgills, whilst to the west, if visibility is good, are the far peaks of Lakeland, including the High Street Ridge where our other fine Roman route heads south on a parallel course.

The farm track continues downhill through a series of sheep pastures (do please close the gates after you) until the track ends at the farmyard of Haber. The public way ends here, and our way is by the metalled lane which leads diagonally down to the dale-bottom. There is a path direct to Low Dalebanks, but a padlocked gate at the end would seem to indicate that the public are not encouraged to use it. On reaching the dale-bottom by the farm road, turn right and a few minutes' walk brings you to Low Dalebanks Farm.

Map 6

The lane is an official bridlepath between Crosby Ravensworth, which lies three-quarters of a mile to the north-east, and the small hamlet of Oddendale. The short diversion to Crosby Ravensworth (which, translated from the Old Norse, means 'the village with crosses at the ford of the ravens') is by this well-maintained bridlepath accompanied along the way by the sparkling waters of Dalebanks Beck, which you cross by footbridge at the edge of the village. The Butcher's Arms is immediately on your right as you enter the main street. The butcher referred to, is Baron John Clifford of Brough Castle, who earned this grim title during the Wars of the Roses for his cold-blooded slaying of the twelve-year-old son of the Duke of York. A notice by the front door advertises lunchtime bar snacks (not open on Mondays) but as yet I have not been able to sample the fare, being on three occasions unsuccessful in my attempts to gain admission (pubs in remote country districts do not always open at lunch-time).

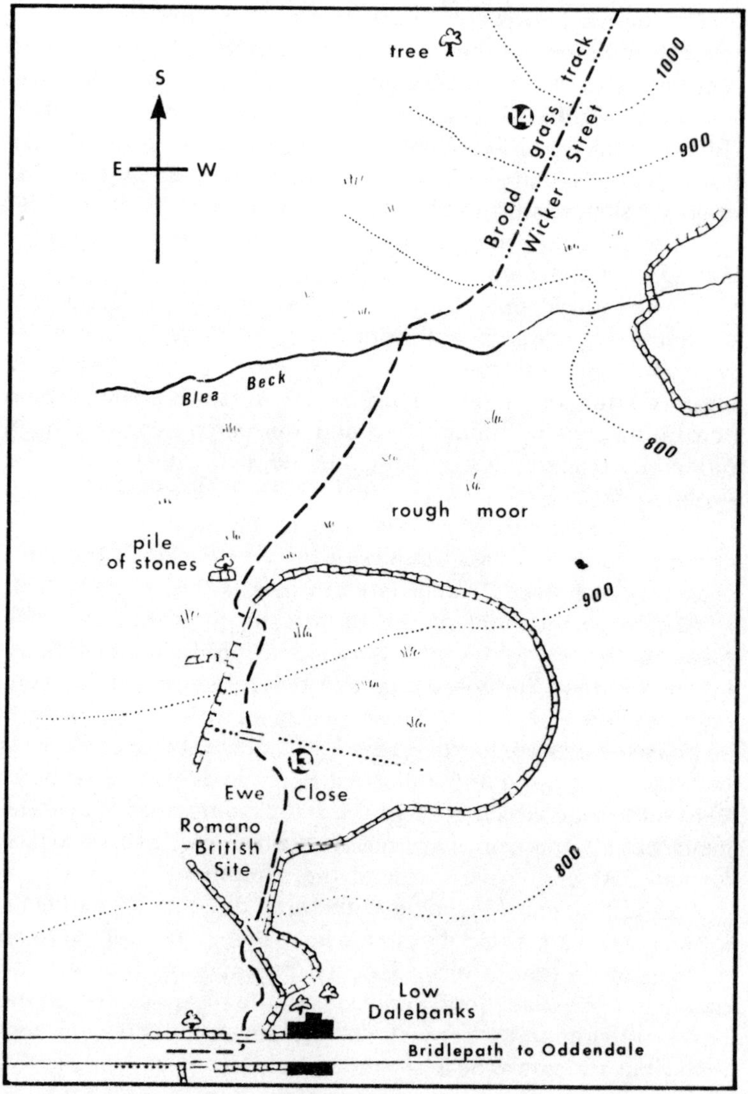
tree
S
E
W
track
1000
14
grass
Street
900
Broad
Wicker
Blea Beck
800
rough moor
pile
of stones
900
15
Ewe Close
Romano
-British
Site
800
Low
Dalebanks
Bridlepath to Oddendale

Map 6

The parish church of St Lawrence, first built in 1190, is reputed to be one of the finest in Westmorland, though, due to restoration work, much of what is to be seen is Early Victorian and mock Gothic. The south porch was designed by Robert Smirke, who was the architect responsible for Lowther Castle, now mainly a ruin – not the best of recommendations. The church holds a large tomb which is thought to be that of Sir Lancelot Threlkeld, the local Lord of the Manor, who married the widow of 'Black-faced' or 'Butcher' Clifford.

On our return, hopefully refreshed, to Low Dalebanks, our way continues southwards, and from this point there is no right of way until the route meets a public footpath across Blea Beck, approximately one mile ahead. There is in fact no defined path across the rough moorland along our alignment, although numerous tracks criss-cross it, but no difficulties should be experienced over this section if the precise directions are followed. Because this is private land, rough as it may be, it is common courtesy to ask permission before crossing it. The close proximity of Lower Dalebanks Farm makes this an easy task.

A gate to the right of the farm leads to a track heading towards the rising ground. After crossing Dalebanks Beck, follow the track through the gate in the dry-stone wall on your right. You are now in Ewe Close, which, as the name implies, is an enclosed pasture for the gathering of sheep and in this case is the site of the large and important Romano-British settlement. Before the wall which borders the track bends right, leave and head uphill between two grass-covered earthworks which formed part of the perimeter of the settlement.

To the trained archaeologist the area must be of particular interest, but I am afraid that to the layman it would appear to be nothing more than a miscellaneous collection of hollows and mounds, and I was, I must confess, a little disappointed on my first visit. Numerous large stones lay about the site, together with what appears to be a large spoil-heap of boulders and rocks.

According to Margary, a section of the Roman road has been exposed nearby, but I was unable to find it, as its precise location is not clear. The Ordnance Survey shows the route passing through the centre of the settlement, whilst Margary places it as passing to the west of the site. Parts of the settlement have been excavated and a number of artefacts found, both Roman and British, giving credence to the theory that the settlement was still occupied when the road was built and which, I think, makes Margary's western bypass much more plausible. The new revised version of the Ordnance Survey Pathfinder Series, sheet NY61/71, shows the Roman route passing along the western side of the complex, and recent aerial photography proves conclusively that the route, clearly identified, does in fact pass the site approximately twenty yards to the west. I have not had the opportunity to seek out the exposed section of road; perhaps the walker may care to do so.

It is more than likely that this large (by first-century standards) native community would have conducted a lively trade with the passing troops, and they can probably claim to be founders of the Cumbrian tourist industry. (It has been estimated that the population of the whole of Britain was at that time between half and 1½ million people.) But now its only inhabitants are a few grazing sheep and numerous rabbits which have made their homes amongst the rocks and banks.

After viewing the site and perhaps trying to imagine the scene as it would have been two thousand years ago, head uphill with the broken dry-stone wall on your left until a wire fence is reached; pass through the gate in the fence and continue uphill, with the wall still on your left, to a gate giving access to the open fell. On gaining the open fell, continue uphill, past a pile of stones along a rough track. Where the dry-stone wall, now on your right, turns west, a solitary tree appears in sight on the far hilltop; this is our (and more than likely the original Roman) sighting point. Aim for a line to the right of the tree across the rough fell; this is important as the track we have been following turns off to the right, and several others cross our route. As the ground levels, look out for a meeting point of two broad tracks; turn right along the second one, which, after crossing the fellside diagonally for a little way, then drops down to the beck in the small valley below. If you miss the meeting point of these two tracks, do not worry: simply head west of the far tree until the ground drops and the beck comes in sight; the track will then be visible.

As we drop down the fellside to Blea Beck, take note of the wide green trackway climbing the right-hand side of the hill ahead; this is the Roman road, still known as Wicker Street. According to Margary, the road crossed the beck by a culvert, the raised approach to which is still visible, as are its stones which lie about. From here on, the walking is easy and the track well defined, as we climb up, just west of the hill summit of limestone rocks, the smooth, broad, grassy track bordered by heather and bracken.

Map 7

Soon after reaching the summit, the track divides into two, which presents the walker with alternative routes. The right-hand route is the more direct and easier, over the shoulder of Coalpit Hill; the left-hand route is over rough ground for a little way until a path is found which leads downhill to Lyvennet Beck and the monument erected to commemorate the fact that in 1651 King Charles II, leading his army south from Scotland, paused here to drink the waters of a shallow well fed by the beck. The fact that he chose to take this route bears witness to the fact that it had been at one time the main route even through to the seventeenth century.

On taking the left-hand path, do not worry if it is soon fragmented into a series of sheep-paths: carry on across the brow of the hill in a south-easterly direction. As the ground begins to dip, a rusty corrugated shed will come into sight in the tiny dale below: this is your target. Heading directly for it, a path will soon be seen leading past the shed to the simple stone pillar with its inscription recording the events of 8 August 1651, less than a month prior to the Royalists' defeat at the Battle of Worcester. The monument was carved in 1843 by Thomas Bland, whose home we passed along our route.

To regain the main route, head up the beck, following the line of shooting butts. Head for the dip in the rough

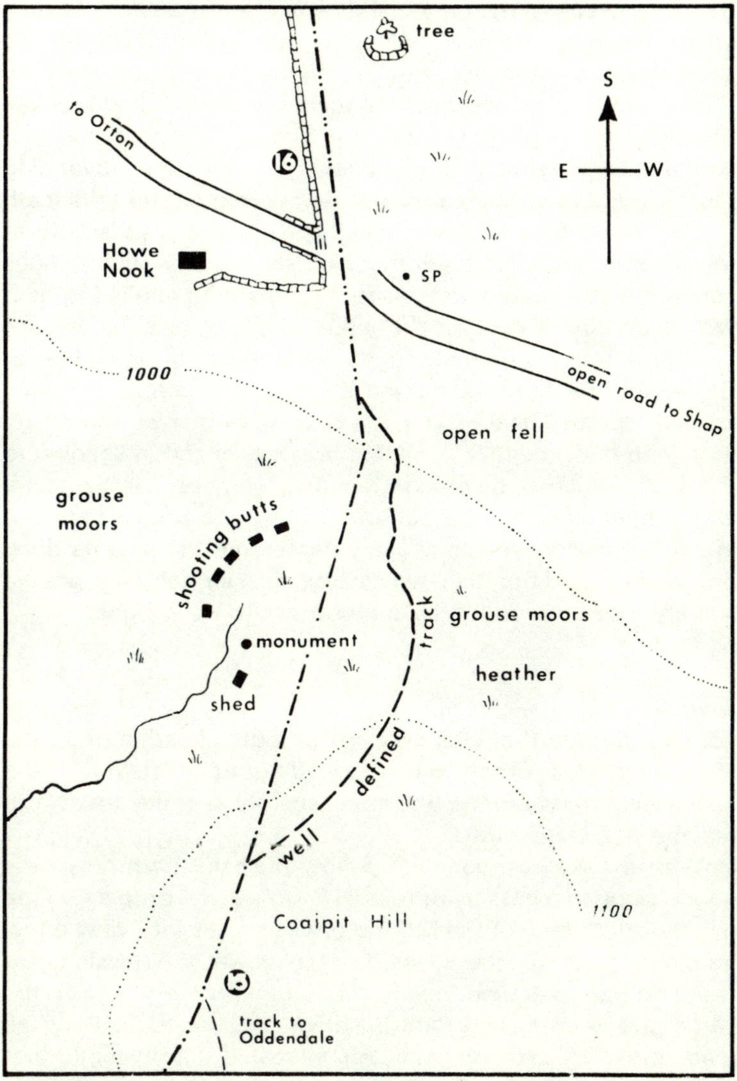
tree
S
E
W
to Orton
16
Howe Nook
SP
1000
open road to Shap
open fell
grouse moors
shooting butts
track
grouse moors
monument
heather
shed
defined
well
1100
Coalpit Hill
15
track to Oddendale

Map 7

heather-covered moor on the skyline, and a further line of butts, where the main track is, will come into sight. When, after a short while, we top the shoulder of the fellside and begin to drop down to the Shap to Orton road, the heather and bracken give way to rough grassland. The Tebay Gap gradually – it would seem reluctantly – opens up for the advancing motorway, and of course for our Roman route. The bridlepath to Oddendale on which we have been travelling ends here at the meeting with the open metalled road. Our way continues across the road and maintains its alignment by public footpath with a dry-stone wall on the left.

It is a mile from here to our next point of reference at Sproatgill, the farm so named on the older maps, but now spelled Sproat Ghyll. The path is very faint over the rough moorland but no difficulty should be experienced in keeping to the route, which is the precise Roman alignment. The dry-stone wall is built along the raised Roman agger, as can be detected in several places, with a shallow depression marking its ditch on the right. About half way along this stretch, we pass a solitary tree surrounded by a stone wall on the right.

Map 8

As we sight a further wall bearing our route ahead, turn off the alignment and cross the moor diagonally towards the south-west to where the wall turns sharply, and we are able to resume our way south.

With the wall on your left, follow the faint path down the gentle slope to a gate by Sproatgill Farm. As you drop down the hill, the south lane of the M6 motorway comes into view a few hundred yards to the west, further down the hillside. On reaching the metalled minor road, turn left and cross the cattle-grid, passing the farm buildings on your left. Along the road, the first gate on your left indicates a bridlepath (not signposted), which, according to the latest Ordnance Survey map, crosses the road to continue south along the original Roman alignment. Indeed a faint track can be detected as it

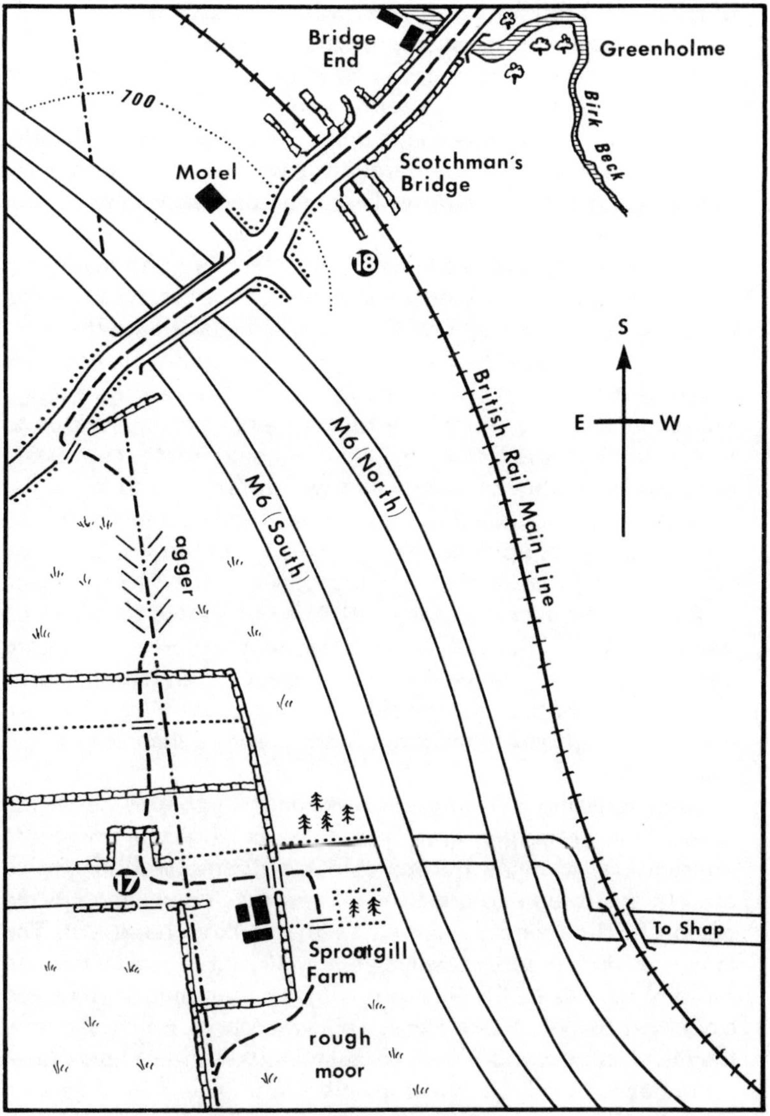
Bridge End
Greenholme
700
Birk Beck
Motel
Scotchman's Bridge
18
S
E
W
British Rail Main Line
M6 (North)
M6 (South)
agger
17
To Shap
Sproatgill Farm
rough moor

Map 8

drops down off the road to what was a gateway in a dry-stone wall; the track can be seen crossing a small field to a similar blocked gateway and thereon to a gate. I do not as a rule advocate climbing over dry-stone walls, but in this case make an exception as the route is definitely a designated bridlepath, and the only possible way around it would be a diversion of nearly two miles. The two walls are low and easy to scale, but be careful to replace any stones displaced.

After crossing the second wall, the track is quite plain as it continues south to a gate in a wire fence; pass through this gate and on to a further broken gate which leads onto the open fell. Here the raised agger is plain to see, with ditches very much deepened by water action as it crosses the rough moorland with the motorway running alongside fifty yards to the west. But soon Roman alignment and motorway clash; progress inevitably conquers, and we are advised to leave the alignment as it approaches a motorway repair tip which blocks the route. A gate uphill to the left gives access to the new road which turns to cross the dual highways of the M6.

As we crossover the motorway, it is interesting to reflect on whether in a thousand years time another breed of *homo sapiens* will be repeating our experience, by wandering down a broad ribbon of crumbling concrete, over grass-filled cracks of an ancient highway many times more obsolete than our Roman roads today.

After crossing the motorway, the lane continues down the fellside on a gentle gradient to cross the main western inter-city railway line by Scotchman's Bridge, well known to the old steam-engine drivers as 'Scottie's Bridge', though the reason for its being so named seems to have been lost. The lane now drops more steeply between dry-stone walls down to the tiny hamlet of Greenholme with the tumbling waters and tree-lined banks of Birk Beck. This was once a busy place: a medieval route and then an eighteenth-century packhorse route passed through, but it is now silent except for a barking farm dog, the only witness to my passing. Through the hamlet, a signpost indicates a lane to Tebay. Near the crossroads a private house gives notice that bed-and-breakfast accommodation is available.

Map 9

The lane to Tebay, for such is our way, climbs up out of the tiny valley; the beck keeps us company below as the lane turns around the hillside. At the top of the hill, a small house in a grove of trees sells milk, eggs and other supplies for the convenience of those using the holiday caravan site beside the beck. The route once more drops to effect the crossing of Bretherdale Beck near its junction with Birk Beck before once more climbing, this time up the slopes of Loups Fell.

On the day of my last visit, heavy, wet cloud enveloped the landscape, making this next mile a little wearisome, but soon after the route begins to drop down the far side of the fell it narrows into a delightful sunken lane between high banks. These are clothed in a rich variety of ferns, mosses and other shade-loving plants, whilst overhead the high, overgrown hedges almost intertwine: even on a dank grey day it was a pleasure to walk along. Soon a small stream joins the lane from the right, and a low white fence separates the two; pussy-willows line the stream, their saffron-dusted catkins brightening the otherwise misty scene. The ancient dry-stone wall on the left and equally old hedges growing out of it bear witness to the long history of this route.

As the lane reaches level ground, the motorway, whose hum we have heard for some time, comes into view, and we know that soon we shall have reached a further stage on our journey south. A bend in the lane and we find ourselves in the old Norse settlement of Roundthwaite, a peaceful oasis, yet so close to the hustle and bustle of modern travel. Like Greenholme, it was once a busy passing place for travellers, packtrains and drovers with their flocks and herds of highland cattle on their way to markets further south. Pre-Reformation there was an abbey here, the lands about being the property of the monks of Shap Abbey, eight miles away as the crow flies. Roundthwaite Beck

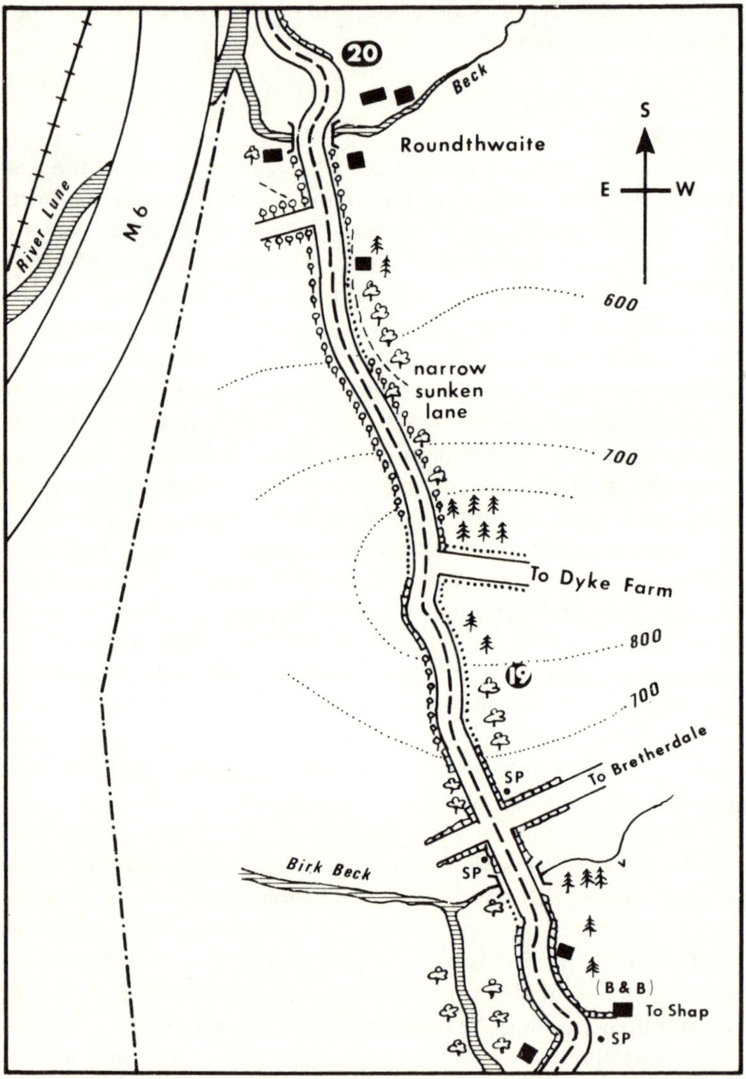
20
Beck
Roundthwaite
S
E
W
River Lune
M 6
600
narrow
sunken
lane
700
To Dyke Farm
800
19
700
To Bretherdale
SP
SP
Birk Beck
(B & B)
To Shap
SP

Map 9

flows through the hamlet on its way to join the Lune as it flows under the motorway.

Leaving Roundthwaite, the now open lane climbs around the shoulder of Jeffrey's Mount, and a fine view of river, railway and motorway is spread out below us with the backdrop of the Tebay Fells above; a thoughtfully provided bench-seat is strategically placed to admire or wonder at the scene.

Map 10

The lane now ends at the junction with the A685 Kendal to Appleby road. Turn right towards Kendal, and just under a mile south a minor road signposted Lowgill leads under the motorway viaduct to the site of the Roman fort at Low Borrow Bridge, the old stone bridge on your left, now completely overshadowed by the more massive modern constructions and used to carry the then only route between Kendal and the county town of Appleby.

Tebay lies two miles north from the fort and about one mile from where the lane joins the main road. It was previously a busy railway halt, being at the junction of the North Western and North Eastern Railway lines, but now only the name of the Junction Hotel remains to bear witness to its past importance. From a food point of view, the traveller is well served, there being a restaurant, the Junction Hotel, which offers accommodation and meals, and a traditional country inn, the Crossed Keys, which extends a warm welcome (an open log fire in winter) and a modest menu of excellent bar snacks; the home-made vegetable soup can be particularly recommended.

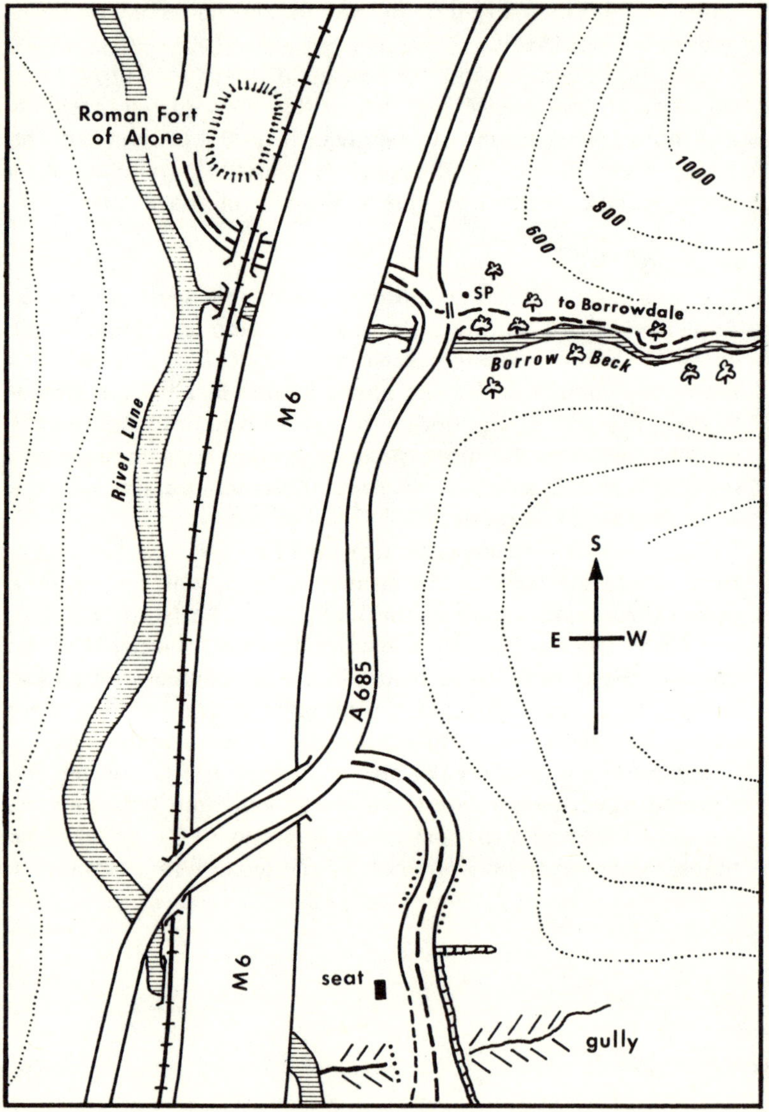
Roman Fort
of Alone
1000
800
600
SP
to Borrowdale
Borrow Beck
River Lune
M6
S
E
W
A 685
M6
seat
gully

Map 10

CHAPTER 2

Low Borrow Bridge (Alone) to Overborough (Galacum). Margary's route 7c. 20 miles.

About the road

The road is a continuation of the main western campaign route described in the previous chapter and covers the twenty miles between the site of the Roman fort of Alone (see note 4) at Low Borrow Bridge and that of the fort of Galacum at Overborough near Kirkby Lonsdale.

The fort of Alone was situated in a typical Roman position at the junction of two rivers, the Borrow Beck, which flows down through the lovely and undisturbed Borrowdale, and the River Lune. The confluence of the two waters, a hundred yards north of the fort, is all but hidden by the massive viaduct which carries the motorway and main-line railway through the Tebay Gap. The fort, originally constructed of turf and timber by the legions of Agricola in AD 79, was probably sited by Agricola himself and was later reconstructed of stone in the reign of the Emperor Hadrian, AD 117–38, although Professor Frere in his joint book *Roman Britain from the Air* suggests that the original Agricolan fort was not at Low Borrow Bridge but further down the valley, near to Sedbergh. He does not expand on his reasons behind this theory and there is no material evidence to support it, but it may explain the controversy over the name.

On the death of Hadrian, the succession passed to Antoninus Pius, who initiated a swift change of frontier policy in Britain. The wall of Hadrian, so painstakingly built, was abandoned, and after the reconquest of the Scottish Lowlands a new turf wall was built across the isthmus between the Forth and the Clyde. In this period many of the Pennine forts were vacated, including Alone, but in AD 158, as a result of trouble with the ever-rebellious Brigantes, many of these same forts appear to have been improved and reoccupied, though there is no evidence to suggest that the fort at Low Borrow Bridge was included.

Our next source of information as to the history of the fort is the *Notitia Dignitatum*, a collection of lists enumerating the chain of commands of the Empire and disposition of forts and forces. Professor Sheppard Frere, from a study of these lists, suggests that the fort at Low Borrow Bridge (he does not commit himself as to its Roman name) was still occupied after AD 369 and that it was probably finally abandoned when Magnus Maximus withdrew his legions in his attempt to gain the imperial crown. The fort was most likely garrisoned by auxiliary troops, a cohort of say five hundred men, who could have been, in later years of the occupation, of British stock.

The road follows a route almost due south for much of the way, keeping to the eastern slopes of the Lune valley on a well-defined course. No doubt because of its excellent construction and gentle gradients, the route has been well used over the centuries, begining with the Norsemen, who used it to penetrate into the fertile Lune valley and to set up their homesteads along its way, as we shall see by the surviving place-names. Drovers used it in part to drive their cattle to the markets of the south. Today, by linking these now quiet country lanes, it is possible to travel the original route for most of its way with ease and comfort, through a countryside rich in history and natural beauty. Diversions from the true route are few and minor and include a fine riverside walk along the River Rawthey and a visit to the Roman milestone at Middleton.

There are several recommended inns of refreshment along the route (timing is vital here), and also excellent overnight accommodation is available at both ends of the walk, indeed at several places along it. The walk can be attempted during all seasons of the year without any special clothing requirements other than a good pair of walking shoes. It is possible to break up the walk into easy stages if you so desire. Sedbergh, reached after a one-mile diversion, offers a moderate choice of accommodation: distance from start approximately eight miles. The Barbon Inn, a further nine miles along the route, and the Pheasant Inn at Casterton (slightly off the route), three miles ahead, are highly recommended, but prior booking is usually necessary.

As well as the guide, the Ordnance Survey Landranger Series Map, sheet 91, should be carried to give a wider view of the area.

The Route
Map 11

We start the walk at the site of the fort (Grid Ref. NY6001), which is situated alongside a small minor road two miles south of Tebay, where, as explained in the previous chapter, accommodation is available. Our road is the first turn left off the A685, which is the old route to Kendal. Immediately after passing under the high viaduct, the fort site of about four acres is the raised ground on your right, its earth ramparts now surmounted by a dry-stone wall. Access to the site is by permission from the adjoining farmhouse, which itself was built in 1827 from stones taken from the south wall of the fort, the western walls being used to construct railway cottages during the building of the LNW Railway. The present owners of the farmhouse, which incidentally started its life as a coaching inn, found evidence of a bath-house outside the fort when, some years ago, improvements were being carried out on the farm buildings.

During the summer months a small number of mobile caravans park in the field immediately below the ramparts, oblivious to their unique camping site.

The site has never been fully excavated, and you cannot help but notice how close both rail and motorway routes pass the

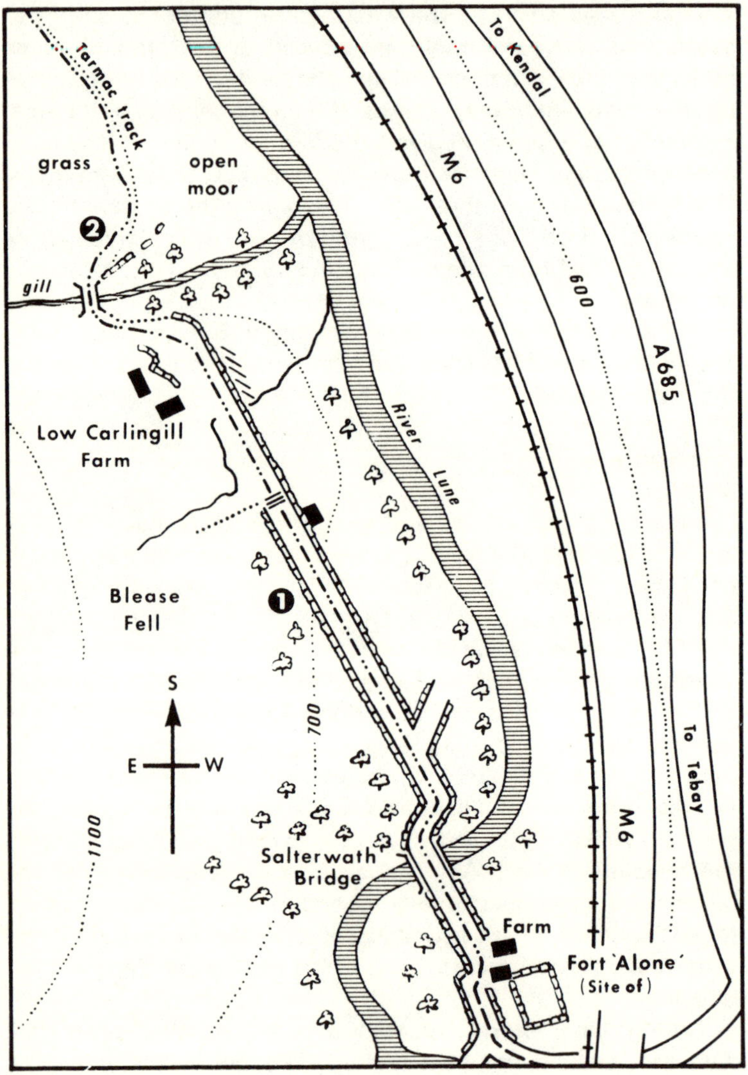
Tarmac track
To Kendal
grass
open moor
M6
2
gill
600
A685
River
Lune
Low Carlingill
Farm
Blease
Fell
1
S
E
W
700
1100
Salterwath
Bridge
To Tebay
M6
Farm
Fort 'Alone'
(Site of)

Map 11

corner of the fort area. We should be thankful that the planners in this instance were able to spare this piece of our heritage. An excellent view of the fort site can be seen by both rail and road travellers, and I always make a point of looking out for it when travelling along these routes.

Leaving the fort site, our way is south along the quiet lane which follows the original Roman alignment to cross the River Lune at Salterwath Bridge, so named after the medieval salt traders whose pack-trains forded the river at this point. After a turn in the road we begin a gentle climb up the lower slopes of Blease Fell, slowly leaving behind the wooded valley to reach the open pastures ahead. Across the valley the fells rise steeply to form a natural amphitheatre which echoes to the hum of traffic and the more strident whistle of inter-city trains as they hurtle down the Shap gradient. The lane is enclosed with dry-stone walls on either side, but after about one mile we cross a cattle-grid and the lane becomes open to the fellside on our left, where a small stream flows down to join us along the way. On the right, behind the wall, evidence of the early agger construction can still be detected.

After passing the farmstead of Low Carlingill (High Carlingill is lower down the fell), the lane does a U-bend to effect the crossing of Carlingill Beck by a small stone bridge, where the waters tumble down the rocky ravine to the river below.

The route now resumes its original alignment, crossing the open moorland on a well-defined terraceway. The smooth, metalled open track makes for good walking, and there is little movement along this ancient way, either on foot or on wheels. In spring sheep and their lamps dot the fellside, their plaintive calls filling the air as grey and white clouds scud across the blue sky. The river gleams its way down the wooded valley, the ground beneath dusted with bluebells. Across the valley, level with our tranquil way, the new mighty highways carry their rushing traffic. Alongside, iron rails vibrate as goods and passenger trains race north and south, but all at a safe distance from the peace and tranquillity of our Roman road, which has endured the ravages of time and man for over nineteen hundred years.

Map 12

This fine open track from the bridge over Carlingill to the cattle-grid ahead, our next landmark, is aptly called Fairmile road, and the cattle-grid replaces what was known as Fairmile Gate. It is indeed approximately a mile between the two points, and the word Fair refers to the fact that in the eighteenth and nineteenth centuries the land alongside the track was given over to an annual gypsy fair, similar to the famous Appleby Fair which of course still takes place. After passing Fairmile Gate and across the cattle-grid, the way once more becomes enclosed between dry-stone walls. This old lane, adopted from the Roman road, for many years served as the main road north from the town of Sedbergh. It is now almost deserted, and it is a delight to walk between its flower-strewn grassy banks, as it meanders south along the contours of the lower slopes of the Howgills.

As the motorway and railway across the valley begin to swing to the west, the high arches of the Lowgill Viaduct comes into view. This proud relic of the bygone age of steam has been long since abandoned. Built by the old Midland Railway Company, it was planned to form a link at Lowgill with the London North Western, but bitter rivalry was too strong, and Midland travellers were often kept waiting for hours before their coaches would be connected with the northern trains. This situation led to the construction of the famous scenic route from Settle to Carlisle, through the heart of the Yorkshire Dales – a route which, alas, has been scheduled to close in the near future.

Three-quarters of a mile from Fairmile Gate and due east of the viaduct, the route passes Gate House, one of several place-names to be found along the way incorporating the word 'Gate'. Derived from the Old Norse word *Gata*, it usually refers to a street or road more than likely of Roman origin. A further half mile of good walking and the route passes a narrow,

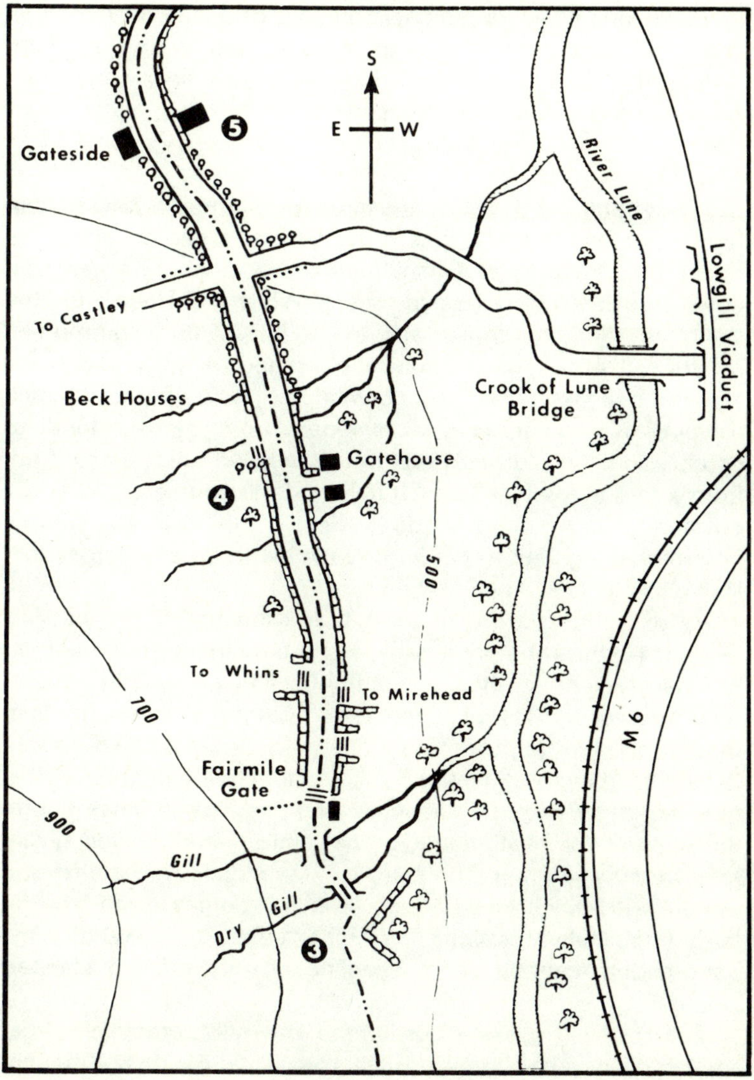
S
E
W
5
Gateside
River Lune
Lowgill Viaduct
To Castley
Crook of Lune
Bridge
Beck Houses
Gatehouse
4
500
To Whins
To Mirehead
700
M 6
Fairmile
Gate
900
Gill
Dry
Gill
3

Map 12

metalled lane which drops down the fellside to the river and the Crook of Lune bridge, not to be confused with the more well-known Crook of Lune bridge at Caton near Lancaster, much praised by William Wordsworth.

Map 13

Our way, still south along the Roman alignment, passes the farmstead of Gateside and turns before dropping down to effect the crossing of Chapel Beck, whose waters cascade down from the high rounded tops of White Fell Head and The Calf, fourteen hundred feet above. The tiny, remote community of Howgill once boasted a school, chapel, smithy and busy woollen mill just a little way downstream; now only the chapel remains in use, drawing worshippers from the surrounding countryside. An old packhorse route crossed here; coming up from a ford across the Lune, it followed the course of the beck, possibly pausing here to do business and visit the smithy before heading east to begin the long climb up and across the Howgill Fells to Kirkby Stephen.

As we climb up out of the gill, leaving the sleepy hamlet behind, we pass the old smithy, a stone building on the corner of a narrow lane on the left; Smithy Beck flows by it. The route now known as Howgill Lane runs straight and true in fine Roman style for approximately one mile and is marked on the $2\frac{1}{2}$-inch survey maps as the Roman road. The River Lune, half a mile to the west, still keeps us company as it flows south through the rich pasture land of the valley bottom, mainly given over to dairy farming. The steep, grassy slopes to the east are dotted with black-faced sheep, and fell ponies roam free in fairly large numbers along the higher fells. At weekends, tiny hang-gliders can be seen wheeling silently off the steeper slopes.

The rounded grassy tops of the Howgills, practically free from walls or fences, make excellent walking country, although care should be taken in misty weather as it is difficult to distinguish between the peaks in such conditions. Due to the slightly off-the-beat situation of the Howgills, they remain

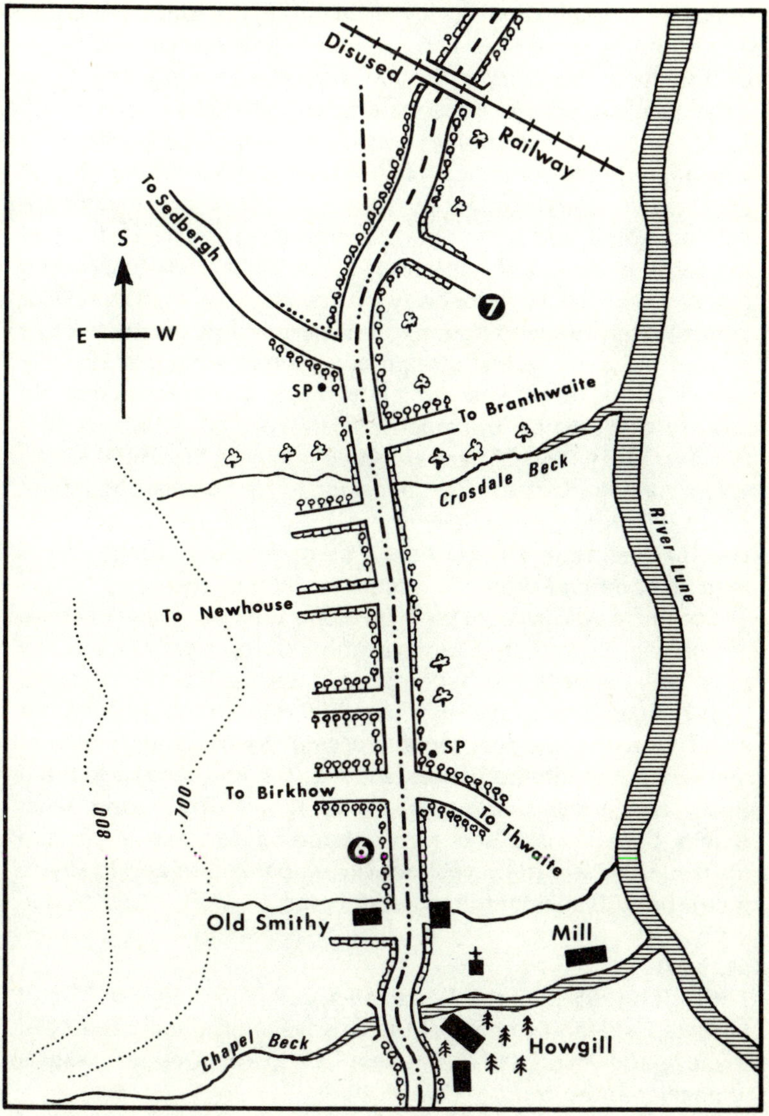
Disused Railway
To Sedbergh
S
E W
7
SP
To Branthwaite
Crosdale Beck
River Lune
To Newhouse
SP
To Birkhow
To Thwaite
800
700
6
Old Smithy
Mill
Howgill
Chapel Beck

Map 13

relatively quiet and undisturbed even during the summer months and in the winter become the solitary man's paradise. Mr A.H. Griffin, the author of many books about the area, comments on what excellent skiing he has experienced on these slopes.

At the end of this straight section of Howgill Lane, the main lane bends left to continue on to the small town of Sedbergh, just over a mile away. Sedbergh (its name, some say, meaning a flat-topped hill and referring to Sadda's Berg 'where Sadda had his fort') is almost a one-street town, its narrow way often blocked with traffic, especially on market day. Fortunately or unfortunately, depending on your view-point, it seems to have missed the main tourist stream and so has remained virtually free from the usual rash of craft shops and restaurants. So beware: don't expect too much in the way of refreshments on a Sunday, for instance. There are three inns, the Bull Hotel which was a halting place for the Lancaster to Newcastle-upon-Tyne coach which began its daily run in 1823, and the Golden Lion and the Red Lion, which offers a comprehensive range of bar food and bed-and-breakfast accommodation.

For those who wish to push on along the route, our way here diverts slightly from the Roman alignment. As already stated, the main lane bends left to Sedbergh; our way is down the narrow, high-hedged lane to the right; the true Roman route is straight ahead between the two forks, crossing the fields in an almost due south direction to join us again at the entrance to Ingmire Back Lane, three-quarters of a mile ahead. The narrow lane, Slacks Lane, twists and turns, dropping to pass under the disused Clapham to Lowgill railway embankment and finally to meet the A683 Sedbergh to Kendal road.

Map 14

Turn left on reaching the A road and pass the gates and drive of Ingmire Hall, family home of the Otways, a prominent family of these parts over the centuries; Sir John Otways was a councillor at the court of Charles II.

The Roman route, coming in from the left, can be identified by the trees which line up with Ingmire Back Lane, which forms

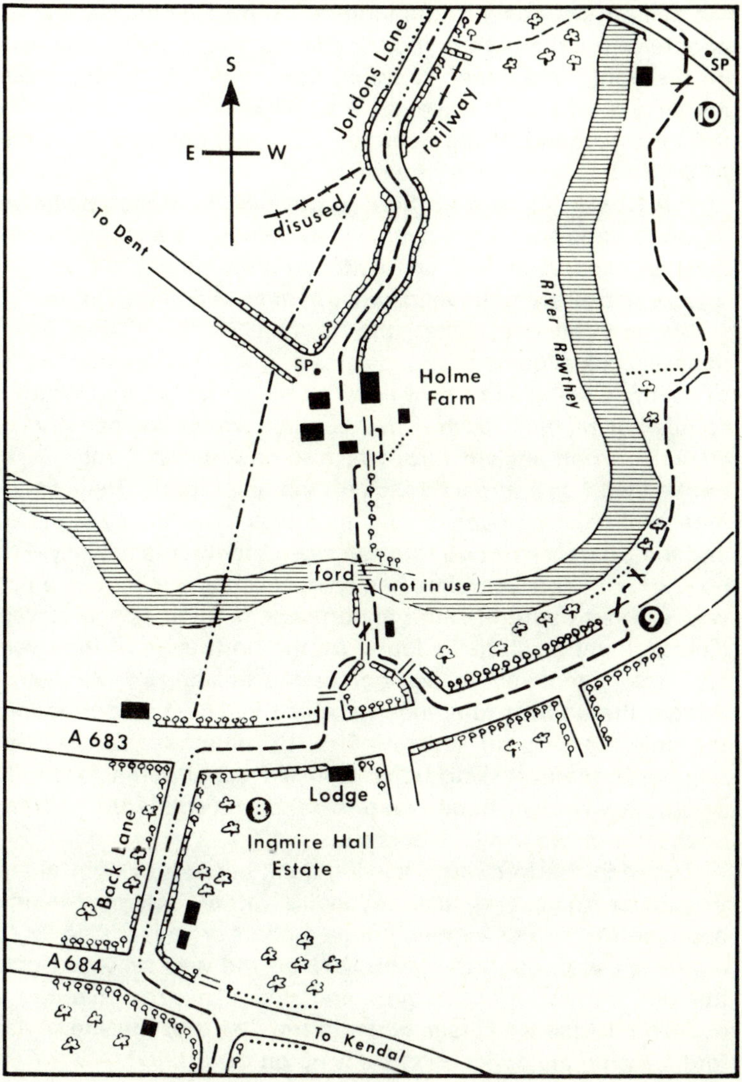
S
E
W
Jordons Lane
railway
disused
To Dent
SP
SP
10
River Rawthey
Holme Farm
ford
(not in use)
9
A 683
Lodge
8
Ingmire Hall Estate
Back Lane
A684
To Kendal

Map 14

the eastern boundary of the Ingmire estate. The pleasant lane, adopted from the Roman road, is bounded by a high stone wall on the right, with banks of spring flowers and bordering trees meeting overhead. It traverses a small hill to drop down onto the lower ground of the Rawthey pastures, before joining the A684 Sedbergh to Casterton road.

The Roman route from here to our next reference point on Jordon's Lane across the river is uncertain and also brings us to our first major diversion, as to effect a crossing of the river it is usually necessary to travel downstream to Middleton Bridge.

Margary suggests that the Roman route at this point maintains its alignment and, on crossing the river, turns slightly to continue along a line now adopted by Jordon's Lane. What is somewhat puzzling is that five hundred yards downstream is evidence of an ancient ford, which is now disused but clearly marked with its approach roads on the older maps. The Roman means of crossing rivers of this type was usually a paved ford, and the existence of two fords so close together is unlikely. For how long the ford at Holme has been in use is not known, but it was without doubt of some importance, judging by the carved direction stone still to be found on the north side of the river; and it was probably in use before the building of Middleton Bridge, the earliest reference to which is 1670, and probably the only crossing for several miles. So whether this was the original Roman crossing point or if the constructed ford was swept away by flood waters and finished up further downstream, we shall never know.

To reach the ford, after leaving Back Lane, turn right along the major road, and just beyond a rather ugly tip, nearly opposite the former Ingmire Lodge a short drive leads down to a gate. Pass through the gate, keeping the wall on your right: the way leads to a further gate and stile. Cross the stile into a riverside field: a wall leads down to the river and the site of the ford, passing the direction stone lying on the ground.

I mentioned previously that a diversion was usually necessary to effect a crossing of the river, and that is so, as there is very little to be detected in the way of a clear crossing, but it can be done if the river water is particularly low after a dry spell and at the risk of a wetting. There is a right of way on the far side which leads through the farmyard and on to Jordon's Lane. But more often than not the ford crossing is impractical and it is necessary to travel downstream to Middleton Bridge. This is no hardship as it is a pleasant riverside walk and generally in the right direction, to pick up the Roman alignment further along Jordon's Lane. Retrace your steps to the stile, here turn left and, instead of crossing over the wall, head for the gate leading to an old overgrown lane which leads up to the main road. This is without a doubt the original route leading to the ford.

On reaching the main road, turn left and proceed along it for approximately half a mile; you will note that the river course draws nearer to the road as you go. Where it reaches its nearest point, look out for a stile half hidden in the hedge – it may be indicated by a footpath sign. A short enclosed path leads to a further stile crossing into a riverside meadow. Follow the river bank as it turns away from the road and heads south. Upstream affords fine views of the Howgill range with the hills of Winder, Crook and The Knott in the foreground, whilst the clear waters of the Rawthey glide quietly over its pebbled bed soon to join the Lune less than a mile ahead. Where a fence is seen to bar your way, head diagonally away from the riverbank to where a foot-bridge passes through the fence and over a small stream; follow a faint path up onto the higher ground where the now high river bank falls steeply down to the river bed. The path leads along the top of the bank to a high stile near a bungalow and then to a stile by the bridge.

Cross the narrow road-bridge: a gate on your left gives access to the wood; follow the path diagonally up the high bank upstream, to cross a small stone foot-bridge over the old railway, onto Jordon's Lane. Here turn right and proceed southwards between its high banks as it drops down to the main road.

Jordon's Lane has been adopted from the original Roman route for most of its length, to a point near Holme Farm. The course of the old railway line runs alongside the lane for some way before crossing the route, to bridge the river three-quarters of a mile upstream from the ford. I had considered using the railway as a means of crossing the Rathey as it is a fine walking route, but a barbed wire barrier across the bridge approaches made this impractical, plus the fact that I was not at all sure about the safety of the bridge itself. I was later to learn, at the inn ahead, that the locals quite often use this route as a short cut to Sedbergh.

Map 15

From Jordon's Lane the route continues along the A683 on the same alignment for approximately one mile, passing on its way the Middleton Fell Inn, earlier known as the Railway Tavern. It dates as an inn from the period of the building of the railway, although the building itself is much older. The inn is the first of several on or near our route, a welcome facility unknown to our Roman travellers. The inn is a free house and as such offers an excellent selection of beers and a good choice of bar snacks at reasonable prices.

Some of my readers may get the impression that this guide in parts sounds like a pub-man's guide to the Roman roads. I make no apology for this, on two counts, one being that the original purpose of the inn was to serve the needs of the passing traveller and the second that there is no better place to pick up interesting bits of local folklore than the country inn. It was here at the Middleton Fell Inn that I heard of the Roman milestone two miles ahead and how the farmer who found it had his name inscribed on it. The details of this I was able to check later at the British Museum.

Hopefully refreshed (opening times can be a little erratic in the winter months), we continue along this straight stretch, with the disused railway on our right. Before crossing under the old railway, the small house on the right is the former Middleton Station. Our next landmark is Middleton Hall, by the junction of the main road and a very much older route known as the Old High Road.

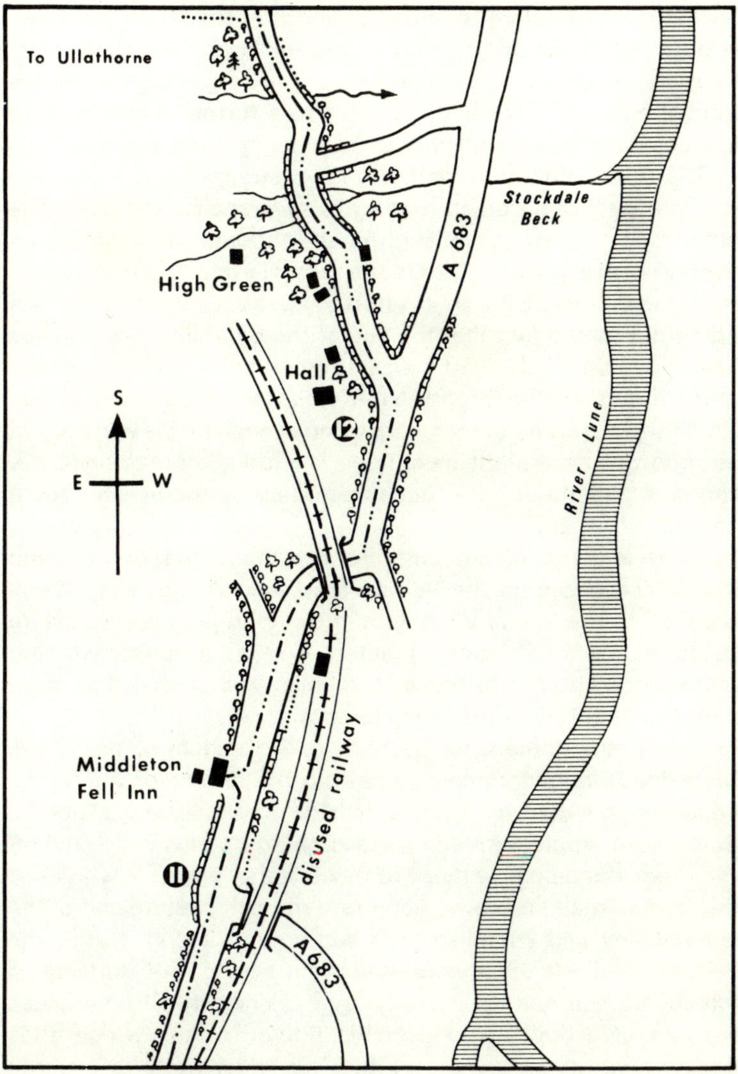

To Ullathorne
Stockdale Beck
A 683
High Green
Hall
12
S
E
W
River Lune
Middleton Fell Inn
disused railway
11
A683

Map 15

It is the generally accepted opinion that the A683 has been adopted from the original route, and this was confirmed so by Margary himself, but I have looked closely at both these routes from the junction at Middleton Hall to a further meeting point just south of Barbon and would like to suggest an alternative.

The A683, the main road, has long, straight lengths, as one would expect of a Roman road, with several dips and rises. The older road, known as the High Road, although maintaining an overall north alignment, bends and twists as it follows the natural contours of the fellside, in its effort to keep a level course. This is borne out by the fact that the line of the old railway, which lies just above the High Road, follows remarkably closely a parallel route. It must not be forgotten that this road was constructed as a military route, and to marching troops consistent levels are just as important as straight lines. There is nothing more tiring than a constant change of pace made necessary by the up-and-down contour of a road.

There is a striking similarity between the situation here and that which exists on the Roman road which leads from Overborough to the fort of Virosidum at Bainbridge in the Yorkshire Dales. As the road leaves Ingleton, it takes a similar winding route along the north side of the valley rather than the more direct route taken by the much later road.

To my mind there is no doubt as to the ancient origins of the High Road: its history can be read in the names of the farms, which in the main lie on the fellside to the east. Eskholme, Sowermire, Applegarth and Ullathorne are names which roll off the tongue and bear witness to those Norse invaders who used the Roman road system to penetrate the rich pastureland of the Lune Valley and establish their settlements along it after the Romans had left these shores. A farm now called Borwens is marked as 'Borrens' on the older maps, a name which indicates the site of a building of possible Roman origin, which adds further strength to my theory that the older route is the true Roman route.

Between Applegarth and Sowermire, an old lane leads off to the right to connect with the main road to the west. This lane is

long. The cylindrical stone is sixty-four inches high and sixteen inches in diameter; the only true Roman inscription on it is 'M.P. LIII', meaning fifty-three miles, this being the distance in Roman miles to the Roman fort at Carlisle. The remaining inscription, 'SOLO.ERUTUM.RESTITUIT. GUL. MOORE. A.N. MDCCCXXXVI.', was cut into the stone by its finder, William Moore, and records the fact that it was found by him and re-erected in 1836. It is assumed that it stands on the line of the Roman route and, looking north, the modern road adopts the alignment for a while to support this theory.

The milestone, although recorded on the Ordnance Survey map of Roman Britain, is not shown on the normal-scale maps – a surprising omission considering the fact that throughout the whole of Britain there have been found only sixty-three milestones, twenty-eight of these in the North of England and Scotland. Whether the fact that it has been 'mutilated' has any bearing I do not know.

After viewing the milestone, return to the High Road via School Lane. Our way continues down the route, now reduced to a one-car width, past those ancient settlements of Applegarth and Sowermire, a delightful walk with little risk of meeting any traffic. The lane, now sunken between high banks, twists and turns, closely following the contours of the slopes of Middleton Fell to the east.

Map 17

On the approach to Barbon village the route crosses Barbon Beck by an old packhorse bridge. Barbon, which was formerly a railway halt, is now left mostly undisturbed, guarding as it does its tiny gem of a dale which lies to the west; a walk through it to Dent is a must to those who are unfamiliar with the area. Turn left on reaching the village. Between the war memorial (recording the two world war losses of the Kay-Shuttleworth family) and the church is the Barbon Inn, highly recommended for its catering. It would be an excellent stopping place for lunch, and bed-and-breakfast accommodation is also available, but prior booking would be advisable. The Italianate Barbon

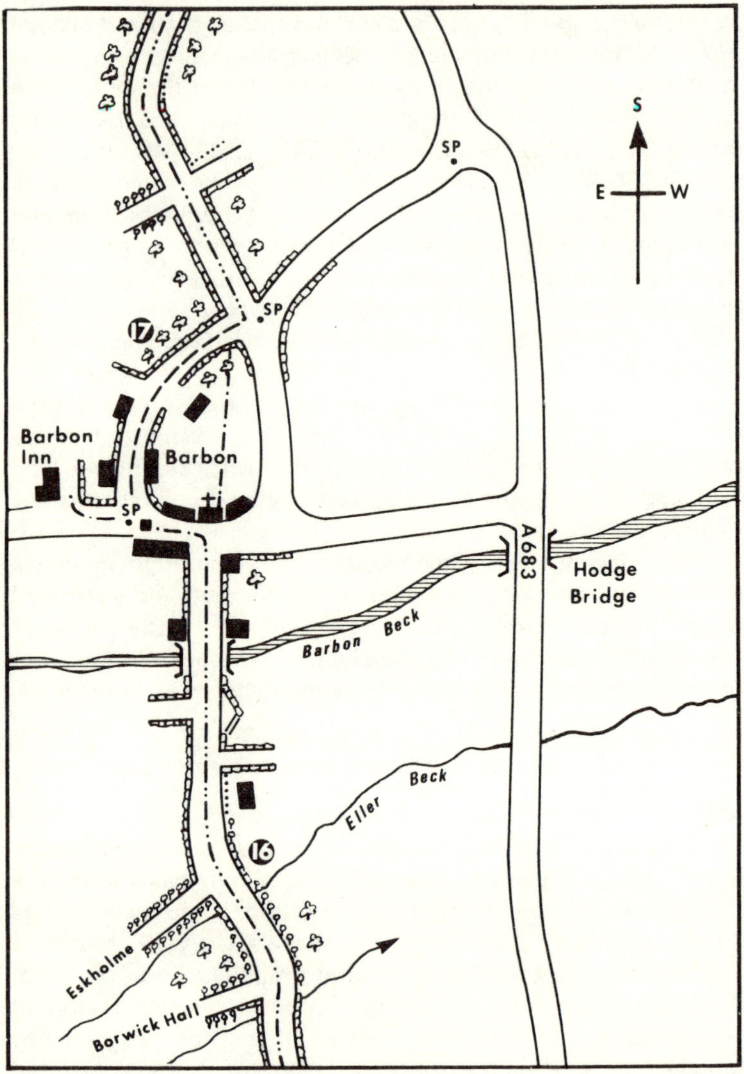
S
E
W
SP
SP
17
Barbon
Inn
Barbon
SP
A683
Hodge
Bridge
Barbon Beck
Eller Beck
16
Eskholme
Borwick Hall

Map 17

Manor lies high amongst the trees of Barbon Fell and was once the hunting lodge of the Kay-Shuttleworths.

If our assumption as to the true course of the Roman route is correct, the road would have passed through where the Wesleyan chapel now stands, and as we proceed along a lane out of Barbon, a long ridge can be seen across the fields to the right, in a direct line with the old High Road. Leave the village by the lane opposite the war memorial, and at the crossroads turn left to resume the undisputed Roman alignment. After passing the lane to Low Bank House, our way bends to the right as it once again joins the old railway route. The true Roman route maintains its alignment across the railway.

Map 18

The lane dops through a wooded area, passing the drive to Whelprigg on the left; a further hundred yards takes us to a small stone barn on the right, our next signpost. Opposite the barn, a gate gives access to a field. Head towards the embankment where a second gate leads to a further gate near a small tunnel under the embankment. Climb up onto the embankment south of the tunnel and continue along it. Many sections of the old railway course have been sold off to private buyers whose lands border the line; this particular stretch consists mainly of gravel chips and would not appear to be of any particular agricultural value – I do not think that British Rail will object if we make use of it for a few hundred yards. Go under the bridge which carries the road crossing the course of the railway; a gate on the left leads onto a metalled lane where we rejoin the Roman alignment. We are now in Wandales Lane, or Wandels Lane as it is now called, but its earlier name was Wanderer's Lane and clearly marked as a Roman road.

After about a quarter of a mile, a lane on the right is the way to the village of Casterton, a short but well worth while diversion. 'Casterton' is translated by some to mean 'the place by the fort', although there is no evidence of such a structure. It is an attractive stone-built village with many interesting features. Its name does indicate some Roman connections, but

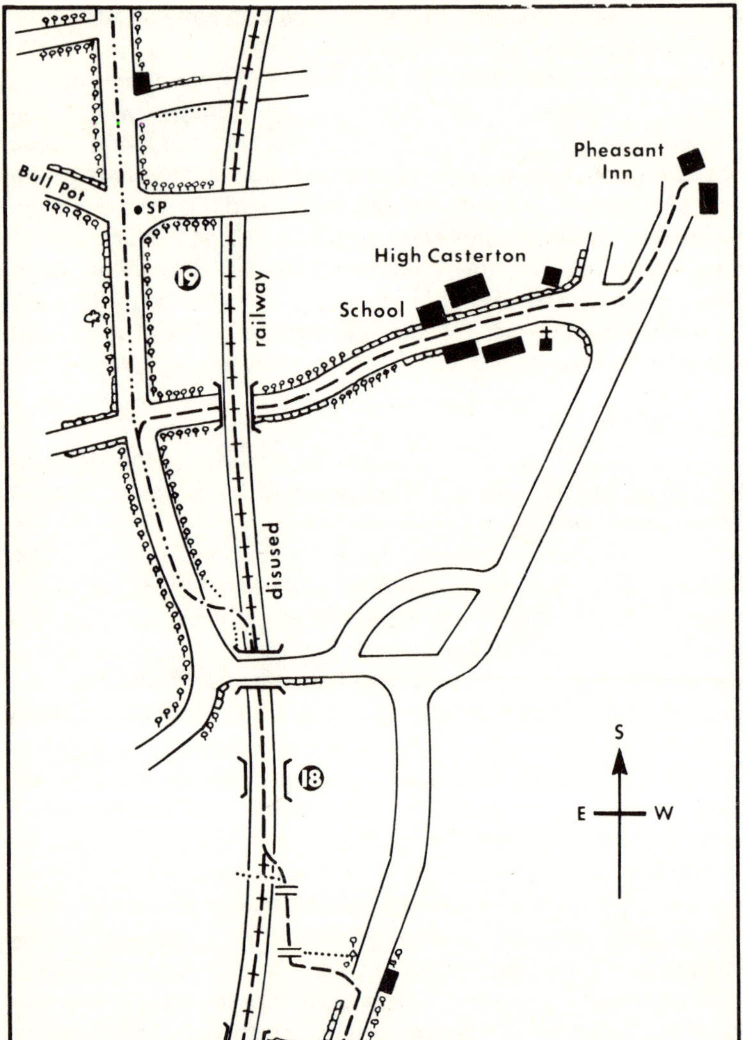
Pheasant Inn
High Casterton
School
Bull Pot
SP
19
railway
disused
18
S
E
W

Map 18

a fort is most unlikely. It has been suggested that there was a Roman glassworks here, presumably using sand from the nearby River Lune. On your way into the village we pass the famous Casterton Public School, formerly a school for clergymen's daughters, founded in 1823 at Cowan Bridge. On the opposite side of the road is the parish church of the Holy Trinity which has the unusual, almost unique, feature of paintings on canvas of biblical scenes, stuck to the walls around the church. On reaching the main road, the A683, turn left to the village and the Pheasant Inn, where a comprehensive range of refreshments can be purchased, ranging from breakfast to morning coffee, and lunchtime snacks to a full evening dinner in the bar or restaurant. The inn also provides excellent overnight accommodation (including a room with a four-poster bed) at competitive prices. It would be advisable to book in the high season if one wishes to break the journey at this point.

I did, earlier in the chapter, comment on the fact that the Romans did not have these excellent facilities, but this is not strictly true. The inn was quite common in parts of the Empire, particularly in towns, but there is no evidence to suggest that there were any established along the roads in the military zone of the north. What they did have was the posting-house and changing station for horses of those officials and messengers travelling by means of the Imperial Post. This system was set up to provide swift communication between the provinces and the Emperor. A normal rate of travel was in the region of fifty miles a day, although faster journeys have been known. Individuals could travel by means of the Imperial Post only if issued with a permit, and these permits were sent out to governors by the Emperor himself. Posting-houses appeared in Britain from late in the first century, and although very few have survived to be identified, it is quite possible that sites along Roman roads with a vague Roman connection (through possibly its name e.g. 'Borrens') could in fact have been used for such a purpose. There are the remains of such a posting-house (or *mansiones* to give it its Roman name), outside the village of High Casterton on Ermine Street in Rutland.

After a visit to Casterton, return by the same route to Wandels Lane along the Roman road. A crossroad sign indicates a lane off to the left to Bull Pot, part of the famous cave system high up on Casterton Fell to the east. Our route, continuing south, lies straight ahead on a gently descending gradient, here known as Long Lane until it meets the A65 (T) main road 1½ miles beyond. The attractive old town of Kirkby Lonsdale lies approximately 1½ miles to the north-west and would make an excellent base as it is well served with all types of accommodation, from the slightly faded elegance of the Royal Hotel to more modest bed-and-breakfast houses. It also has a good choice of cafés and restaurants of a high standard and an interesting selection of quality shops. A nearer source of refreshment is the Whoop Hall Inn just a third of a mile towards Kirkby Lonsdale; the home-made bar snacks are well above average.

Map 19

From the junction with the A65 (T), the Roman route for a few hundred yards has been adopted by the main road as it maintains its almost due south alignment; where the modern road turns left towards the village of Cowan Bridge, the Roman route continues down a farm lane. The lane bends left and crosses a small beck; the true route continues across the field, but we follow the lane through High Gate Farm (note the significance of the name) to a walled lane which leads down to Leck Beck. Turn right and follow the beck downstream to a footbridge. The Roman road crossed the beck by a paved ford slightly upstream from the bridge, and some evidence of this can still be seen. The Roman fort of Galacum (Grid Ref. S.D.6175) was sited one mile downstream to the west near where the Leck, previously known as the Lac, joins the Lune at Overborough, or Overborrow as it is sometimes called.

Not a lot is known about the fort, as the site is partly covered by the Georgian mansion of Over Burrow Hall, built in 1740,

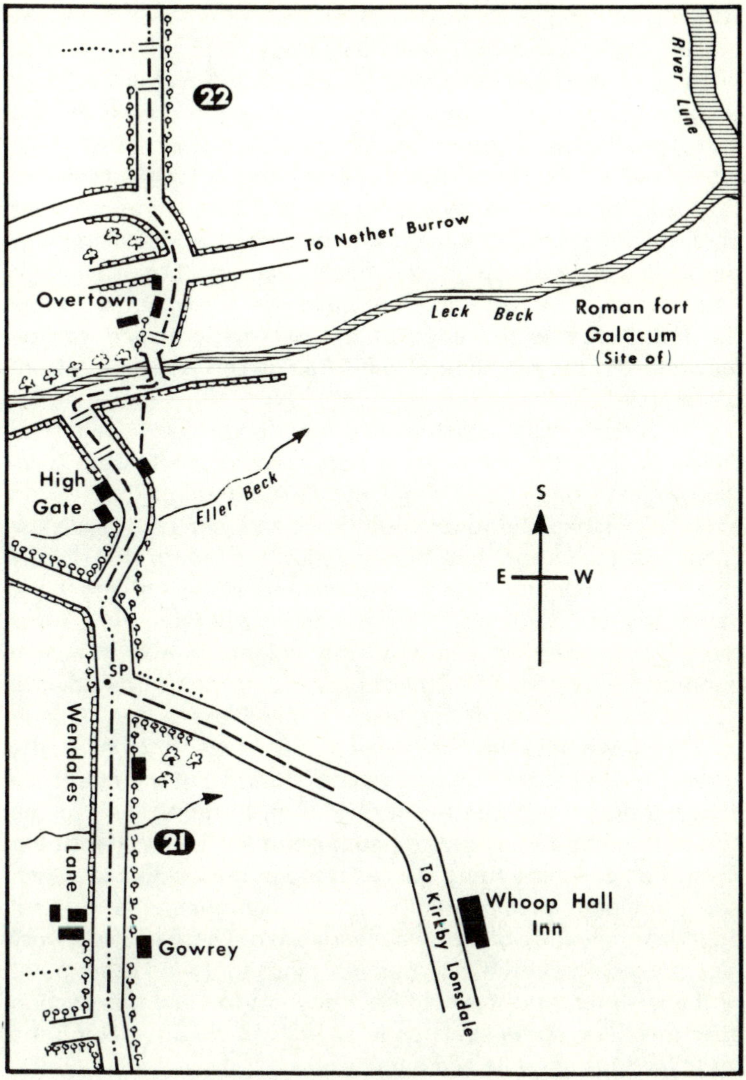
22
River Lune
To Nether Burrow
Overtown
Leck Beck
Roman fort
Galacum
(Site of)
High
Gate
Eller Beck
S
E
W
SP
Wendales
Lane
21
To Kirkby Lonsdale
Whoop Hall
Inn
Gowrey

Map 19

when early antiquaries made several finds of interest, but many of these have since been lost. One stone does survive, having been built into the north wall of the church at Tunstall, inscribed with an epitaph to a camp doctor invoking the godess Hygeia and Aesculapius. Another sculptured stone can be seen built into a barn on the roadside a few yards north of the entrance to the Hall. The latest excavations were in 1950, when evidence confirmed that the fort dated from the time of Agricola and was probably occupied up to the fourth century, but nothing is known about the fort's internal buildings. A slight rise below the Hall indicates the edge of the fort platform and can be viewed from the roadside of the A683 which passes the front of the Hall.

The branch road which would have connected the fort of Galacum with the main route north would most likely have followed the beck down from the ford, although there is no evidence visible. The route south from here comes outside the scope of this book but briefly follows a south to slightly south-east alignment down the eastern slopes of the Lune valley until the Bowland Fells are reached. Here the route turns more south-west to climb to the height of over fourteen hundred feet across the Bowland moors; it then turns down a natural route between the hills to negotiate some difficult terrain, down into the valley of the Hodder. It crosses the Hodder twice before it reaches the sighting point of Jeffery Hill at Longridge, finally, with a further turn, to drop down to the site of the Roman fort of Bremetennacum at Ribchester on the River Ribble. As the route passes through marginal land which has remained uncultivated over the centuries, the original agger can, in many places, be clearly seen. There is also a very well-preserved stretch of agger very close to the finishing point of this chapter, and it would be a pity not to view this section after travelling so far towards it, so we will continue along the route for a further mile and a half.

After crossing the Leck Beck, our way is through the tiny hamlet of Overtown. Turn left up the main but narrow lane, the true route seen as a line of trees on the left of the lane. Where the lane turns sharply, our way maintains the alignment down a rough lane between hedges (this can be very muddy in wet weather). The rough lane crosses a small hill to drop down to a gate which leads into a field: continue through the next gate and further stile.

The indication of an agger can now be clearly seen, the wall on the right marking the line. A small stream crosses the route, but a short diversion to a foot-bridge by a fallen tree overcomes this. The route is now blocked by the swift-flowing Cant Beck, so move upstream to a concrete foot-bridge hidden in a grove of trees. A courtesy call at the farm just nearby, called Collingholme, is advised as this is private land.

Return to the beck, go downstream and regain the original alignment through a gate in the fence; here you will see what is probably the finest stretch of undisturbed agger to be found in the north-west – approximately sixteen feet wide and standing three feet high above the surrounding ground. Mr Watkins, in his book on Roman Lancashire of 1883, comments that 'the ground here about was moist and sedgy and had never been furrowed by the plough' – the same conditions would appear to apply equally today, a hundred years later, but for how long, I wonder. The agger remains prominent for a good quarter of a mile. It would be interesting to investigate further and, by correct excavation procedure, discover the precise details of its construction, types of material used etc.

The walker can now retrace his steps to the minor road which, on turning right, leads to the village of Cowan Bridge. Just by the road-bridge over the Leck is the former small private school attended by the Brontë sisters; a plaque records the time and place. If you wish to continue a little further, follow the alignment up the small hill ahead; beyond here the Roman route has been adopted for a short way by a narrow lane; continue down the hill – a slight detour is necessary to cross a small stream. To your left, on a hill, is Scaleber Farm, another name often associated with Roman remains. From the farm, a metalled lane leads to the A687 less than a mile from Burton in Lonsdale, where refreshments can be obtained at the

Running Pump Inn in the centre of the village. Other routes can be taken which lead to Tunstall and Cantsfield to the west and south.

CHAPTER 3

Low Borrow Bridge (Alone) to Watercrook (Alavana). Margary's route 707. 8 miles.

About the road

This road was constructed as a branch route, off the main north–south road along which up to now we have been travelling, and was built to connect the fort at Watercrook, south of Kendal, with this main supply route. Its Roman name has now been firmly established as Alavana. The dating of roads can sometimes be difficult and is in this case, but as the fort at Watercrook was not built until early in the second century, it would be fairly safe to assume that the connecting military road was constructed about the same time. The first two miles of the route from Low Borrow Bridge are involved in the steep climb up to Grayrigg Common and the radio station, with splendid views of the charm of Borrowdale stretching to the north-west. Over the ridge the little visited, or even known, pasturelands of Grayrigg and the valley of the River Mint spread out below and before us, whilst in the far background the high Lakeland peaks dominate the horizon.

The climb to the ridge is in parts boggy, so good footwear is necessary, but from then on the route is very easy to follow down a gentle gradient, along delightful lanes banked with flowers. To get the maximum enjoyment out of this walk, I suggest a bright clear day in early spring as the ideal time, although for those who like winter walking there is no reason why it may not be undertaken, providing the visibility is good.

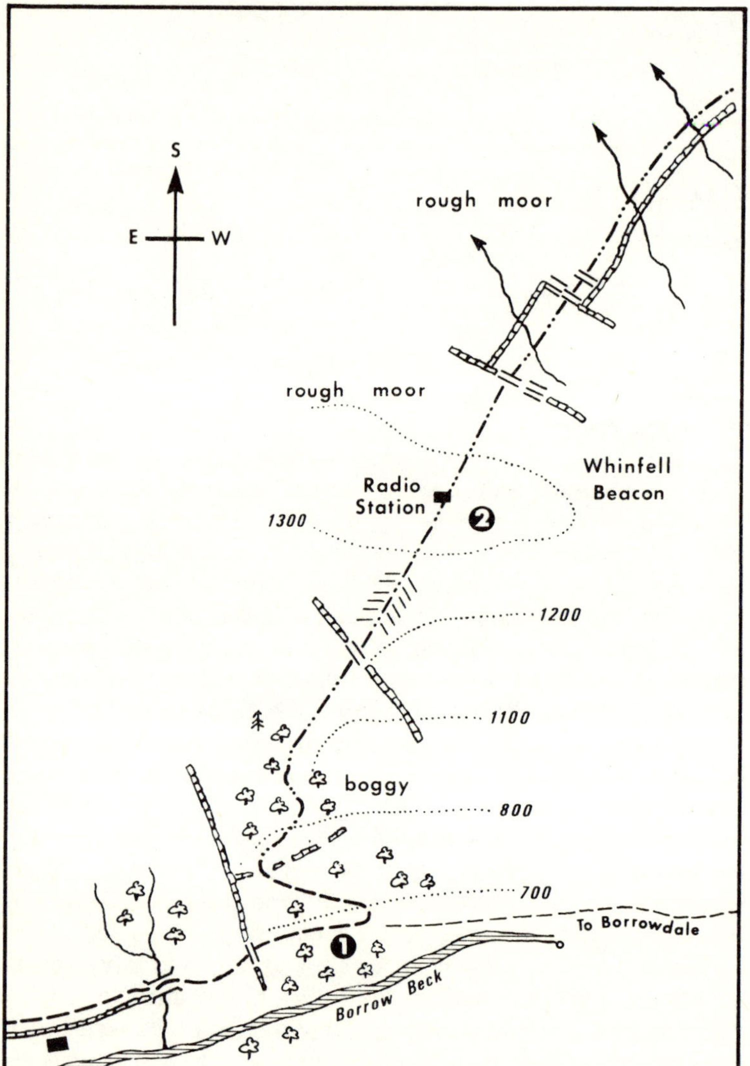
S
E
W
rough moor
rough moor
Whinfell
Beacon
Radio
Station
1300
1200
1100
boggy
800
700
To Borrowdale
Borrow Beck

Map 20

The Route
Map 20

We leave the fort site at Low Borrow Bridge (fully described in Chapter 2), going under the viaducts to the A685. Cross the road to a small car-park and the entrance to Borrowdale; a signpost indicates the track to High and Low Borrowdale farms. Proceed along the wooded track, where the beck flows alongside. After a stone barn, cross a bridge over a small stream which flows down the steep slopes on the left; the track now is open either side. Shortly after passing through a gate which lies across the track, a rougher track leads off to the left, turning back on itself to wind its way up the fellside through a small plantation of trees: this is our way.

After passing through a gateway in a ruined dry-stone wall, the now faint track makes its way up the fellside in a generally south-west direction. The ground here can be boggy even in dry weather and the track difficult to follow precisely, but as it clears the trees it becomes much more clear, and the broad turf strip marks the base of the old Roman road. Passing through a gate, the route of the road is clear to see and easy to follow over the rough open fell. The radio station is now in sight directly ahead on the brow of the hill, and looking north-west, much of Borrowdale, with its beck winding its way through it, lies below us. The dale has for some time been under the threat of being turned into a reservoir but public opinion will, we hope, prevent the drowning of what is considered to be one of the prettiest of the Cumbrian dales.

The rather ugly radio station owned by British Telecom is a radio repeater station, unmanned and used for boosting messages over the hills, and it appears to sit fair and square across our ancient route. Skirt around the station to where the concreted path now descends the slopes of Whinfell.

Margary describes the Roman road as a broad green track continuing its south-west alignment down the fellside. Later writers' descriptions of the area refer to the concreted path (constructed by the then GPO and designated a private road but also a public footpath) as following the line of a much more ancient route, and it would seem likely that it does indeed for most of its way adopt the Roman alignment, and covers the original construction.

Immediately due west of the station is Whinfell Beacon, the second highest point on the Whinfell Ridge at 1,544 feet. It is one of a system of official beacons established to give warning of Scottish raiders and is included in a list dated 1468. The grove of trees on the south-west slope was planted to provide fuel. For those who do not mind the extra effort, the beacon can easily be reached from the radio station, with very extensive views to the south and west as a reward. A gate in the dry-stone wall on the northern slope on a level with the station gives access to the summit.

From the start of our continued journey down into the valley of the Mint, the way maintains its south-west alignment and indeed continues to do so, allowing for twists and turns, for the entire route to Kendal. As the track begins its gentle descent diagonally down the fellside, it is at first unenclosed, but after passing over a cattle-grid the way is accompanied by a dry-stone wall, first on the left and then, after a further cattle-grid by a double set of gates, on the right.

Map 21

The track continues to descend over a series of cattle-grids and small streams which cross under the track by culverts, and on warmer days cattle can be seen high on the slopes of Whinfell, a clear sign of good weather ahead. Where the track becomes enclosed between hedges, the ground levels out for a while and the rough fell, over which we have been passing, gives way to green pastures dotted with numerous sheep, in places dusted yellow by the bright petals of celandines basking in the spring sunshine. The track drops once more down to the gate which gives access to the metalled lane. Here we turn right, when, after about a third of a mile, a small crossroads is reached. It is possible that the lane on the right, to Cockin, follows the original route, as here we turn left to continue the alignment. We drop slightly before climbing a small hill, the now banked

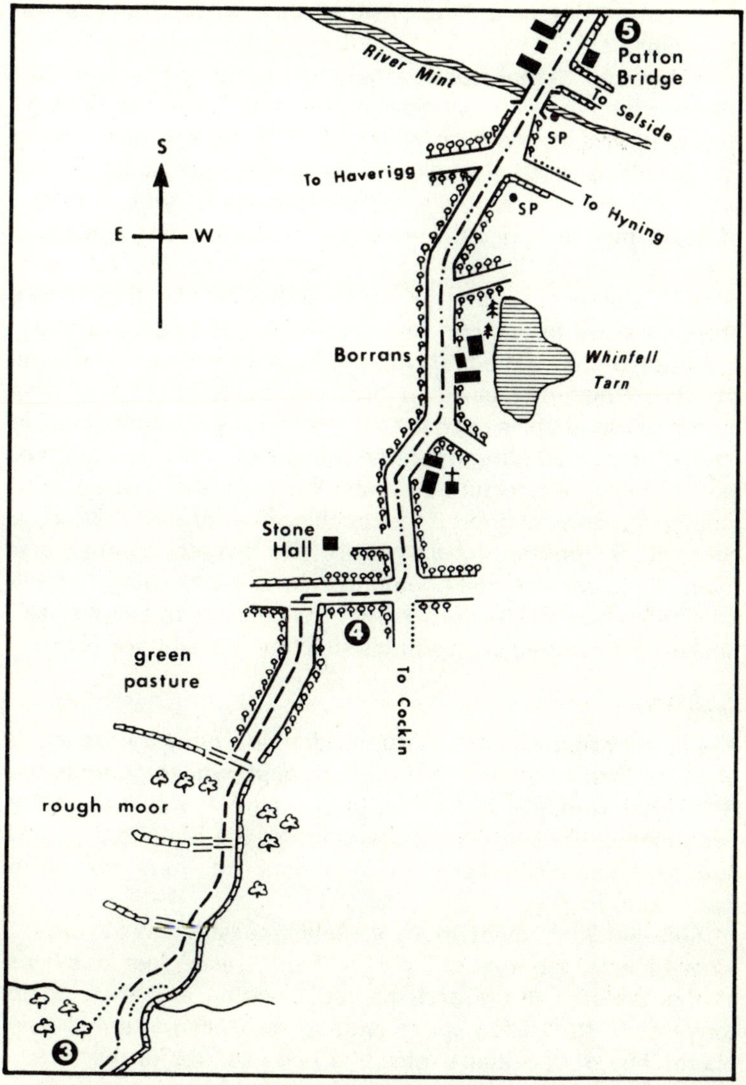
River Mint
5
Patton
Bridge
To Selside
SP
To Haverigg
To Hyning
SP
S
E
W
Borrans
Whinfell
Tarn
Stone
Hall
4
To Cockin
green
pasture
rough moor
3

Map 21

lane, on the day of my last visit, brilliant with primroses and celandines.

A deserted chapel stands empty and silent as the lane once more continues its overall descent. Whinfell Tarn lies nearby on the right, behind the farm buildings of Borrans, a place-name which tells us much of its Norse origins and even earlier Roman past – the site of a Roman staging-post perhaps, with a change of horse for the imperial messenger before tackling the climb over Whinfell on his way north. From Borrans, the way runs straight and level for approximately a quarter of a mile before dropping once more down to the River Mint and Patton Bridge.

Patton Bridge is the first community settlement so far met as the River Mint travels down this remote valley. At one time numerous small mills used the waters for power, some of which have disappeared altogether, the remainder converted to other uses, mainly domestic, as they were mostly cottage-size employing only two or three people. The one at Patton, a cornmill, is reputed to date from the twelfth century and remained in use until the twentieth; it is now a dwelling, the mill race still remains. The settlement now consists of half a dozen houses, a converted blacksmith's shop and a telephone kiosk.

Map 22

The lane climbs up from Patton Bridge and turns by the lodge of Shaw End, an elegant mansion, through whose grounds the River Mint wanders to the east of our route. It was built in the early nineteenth century, as the home of the Shepherd family, and its façade can be seen at a distance from the A685 Grayrigg road.

Still climbing, even more steeply, the lane finally tops a small hill near the road to Field End Farm. Take a last look back at the Whinfell Ridge and the radio station and then again forwards to the rolling countryside, generously patterned with plantations of deciduous trees and rich pastures of the widely scattered farmsteads, a sign of the ancient security and peace of this hidden valley. Names such as Skelsmergh, Scalthwaiterigg, Goodhamseales, and Dockergarths, amongst others,

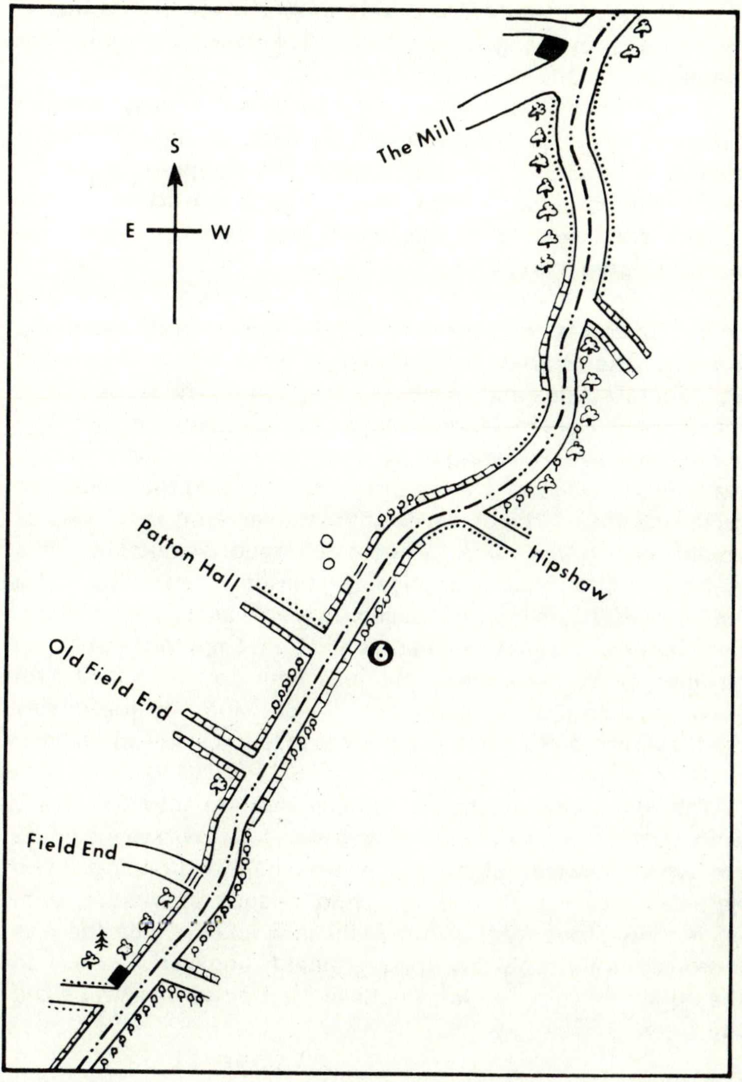

Map 22

bear witness to the early Norse settlers who made their homes in the fertile valley. Range upon range of Lakeland peaks dominate the skyline to the west and north.

An earlier chapter made reference to the heavily wooded nature of the territory of these northern parts of the province and indeed of Britain in the early days of the Roman occupation. Whilst this is generally true, it has now been accepted that considerable clearing of the woods and forests which once covered a great part of the countryside had already begun by the late Iron Age. In the south, for instance, where the growing of grain crops was developed to a very high degree under the Romans, the Britons had already a quite highly developed agricultural society and an export trade of grain and cattle across the Channel. Here in the north a growing population would have led to the gradual clearing of the woodlands along the slopes of these fertile valleys for the growing of grain and the feeding of cattle and sheep. The presence of the Roman army in the district would have done much to boost this food production, for it consumed enormous quantities of grain (it is estimated that a legion needed five hundred bushels a week) as well as substantial quantities of meat, vegetables and fruit. Even today this long tradition of cattle-rearing continues with some 58,000 beef cows producing a calf every year for growing into top-quality beef, many to be found in small herds in farms in hill and upland parts of the county.

The lane now begins its gradual descent into the valley amongst lush green pastures. The ground falls away to the left as we wend our way along the hillside before dropping down between high banks and flowering hedges alternating with ancient dry-stone walls. A turn in the lane takes us due south as it drops more steeply down, the ground falling sharply away on the right, whilst on the left the River Mint flows unseen behind the trees.

Map 23

A lane on the left indicates the way to the mills and small industrial estate of Meal Bank. The village is hidden behind

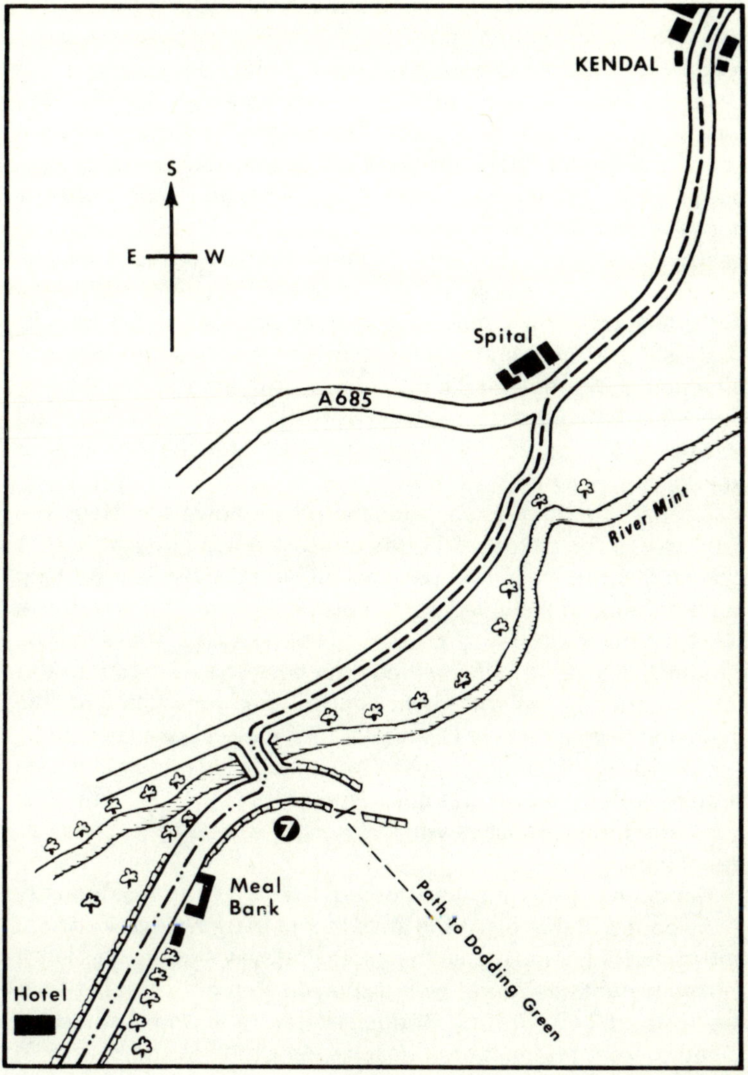
KENDAL
S
E
W
Spital
A685
River Mint
7
Meal
Bank
Path to Dodding Green
Hotel

Map 23

trees in a deep hollow by a bend in the river and can be reached by a minor road leading off to the left a few yards beyond the mill road. Our way continues along the main lane passing the Laverock Hotel with its public bar and catering. Shortly after passing a small housing estate we meet the River Mint as it comes in from the left on its tree-lined course at Laverock Bridge, its graceful arch spanning the tranquil, shaded stream. Directly opposite the bridge on your right, a public footpath leads to nearby Dodding Green, with its small Roman Catholic chapel, formerly a private house; it was left to the Church in 1723, and the gravestones of some of its earlier priests can be found.

Cross the river and continue in the same south-westerly direction along the hedged minor road until after approximately three-quarters of a mile it meets the A685 Kendal to Tebay road at Spital. A further mile along this road and the outskirts of Kendal are reached.

Kendal is a busy town, with the proud boast of being 'The Gateway to the Lakes', although a new bypass now carries the Lakeland traffic speeding past on the west. Even so, the long main street is still choked with vehicles in spite of the one-way system which seems to cross the river several times before directing the traffic in its desired direction. The A6 and the A65 routes converge on the town, and rail link connects with the main north–south line at Oxenholme. The town is well served by a wide variety of eating houses from the humble fish and chip shop to coffee shops, cafés and restaurants as well as numerous pubs and hotels, most of which cater for the hungry as well as the thirsty.

Kendal has two museums, one of Lakeland Life and Industry in the centre of the town, and an older but extremely well laid out and more traditional museum near the railway station. This latter museum contains many well-displayed Roman artefacts from the forts at Low Borrow Bridge, Watercrook and Ambleside, together with an illustrated description of life in the district in Roman times.

The site of the Roman fort of Alavana at Watercrook (Map Ref. S.D.5190) is just about a mile south of the town, strategically placed with three sides surrounded by the bend in the river, and although there is very little to be seen on the surface today, considerable excavations have taken place and many finds been made, including a temple block dedicated to P. Aelius Bassus, an ex-centurion of the Twentieth Legion, together with many fragments of pottery and glass.

The fort covered an area of just under four acres and was probably manned by five hundred auxiliary troops (see note 5). The ex-centurion of the Twentieth Legion, previously mentioned, could very well have served at Alavana in command of the auxiliary garrison at one time or another, a quite common form of detached service undertaken by centurions of the legions in Britain, which is well recorded.

CHAPTER 4

Brougham Castle (Brocavum) to Troutbeck (Ambleside). Margary's route 74. 20 miles.

About the road

The road which we are to follow was constructed to connect the Roman fort of Brocavum, at Brougham Castle near Penrith, with the Lakeland fort of Galava situated south-west of Ambleside. To give a precise date to the construction would be impossible, but we do know that the fort of Brocavum was built by Agricola in the years AD 80–81. There is also evidence that Galava was built somewhere between AD 90 and 100, so that it would be fairly safe to assume that the road was built in that latter period.

The route is, in some respects, an unusual Roman route, for it involves itself in a great deal of mountain-climbing, passing for many miles along its way at a height of over two thousand feet. Ivan Margary, in his description of the route, questions the necessity of such a high-level road, but I think that anyone familiar with the complexity of the topography of the region, with its deep valleys and craggy slopes, will agree that the Roman surveyors did an excellent job when they planned this route. Even today, with the modern road system, it represents the walker's shortest route between the two points, a remarkable achievement through this wild and broken landscape. It has also been suggested that the Romans simply adopted an already existing ancient tribal hill track – this was not unknown where it suited their purpose. If they did, they would then have adapted it to their own high standards. Excavations some years ago firmly established its Roman construction.

Because of the cultivation and development of the farmland in the immediate area near the fort, the first few miles of the route have been lost, so that our way is mainly along country lanes which are none the less interesting as they pass through a region rich in history and Arthurian legends. It is not until we reach Winder Hall Farm, approximately five miles along the way, that we can finally consider ourselves to be on the true Roman route.

From this point the route climbs slowly but steadily upwards along a long spine of hills until the height of 2,700 feet is reached. It is a magnificent walk with some of the finest views in Britain to be seen in every direction. Once on the high hills it is not practical to break off the walk; descents into the deep valleys which radiate from the ridges are lengthy, sometimes confusing, and can often be dangerous to those unfamiliar with the region.

Nevertheless, it is not a difficult walk if sensible precautions are taken and suitable clothing and footwear worn – do not forget that a warm day in the valleys can become bitterly cold at two thousand feet. In the hot summer months dehydration can be a problem if no water is carried as there is an eleven-mile stretch without shade or running water. In calculating the time needed to complete the route, do take into account that much of it is uphill and there is no way that you can stride along at the regulation Roman army pace of twenty miles in five hours – I suspect that, along this route, neither did the Romans.

An early start to the hardest part of the route can be achieved by staying overnight at the Queen's Head Inn at Tirril, 3½ miles from the start. The comfortable eighteenth-century inn has great character and a friendly atmosphere.

As well as the guide maps, the Ordnance Survey Landranger Series Map, sheet 90, should be carried to give a wider view of the area and surrounding countryside, and I strongly recommend *The Pictorial Guide to the Lakeland Fells*, Book 2, by A. Wainwright, a splendid little book which gives valuable information regarding the many surrounding peaks and mountain ranges which I would find it impossible to include.

The Route
Map 24

The site of the Roman fort of Brocavum is described in detail at the beginning of Chapter 1, lying as it does in the shadow of Brougham Castle, one mile and a half south-east of Penrith (Grid Reference NY3728).

You will note that the dry-stone wall surrounding the site is constructed in part of very regular stone blocks which most likely were quarried and cut by the Roman legionaries in the first century when the fort was rebuilt, probably in the reign of the Emperor Hadrian. I am afraid our forefathers were not so concerned with preservation as we are, as is also clearly shown by the reduction of so many of the Pennine forts as well as Hadrian's Wall itself.

We leave the site of the fort and proceed down the B6262 in a south-westerly direction, the quiet country lane following the general direction of the original route. Soon after passing a small housing estate on the left, we are faced with what appears to be a medieval castellated wall and gateway which bridge the lane to a small chapel, half hidden by a grove of trees. The gateway and wall are all that remains of Brougham Hall, largely built between 1830 and 1840; it was sold and demolished in 1934, and parts were used to build a restaurant near Appleby. The hall was part of the estate of Henry Peter Brougham, Lord Chancellor from 1830 to 1834, 1st Baron of Brougham and Vaux, whose other claim to fame – the one for which he is remembered – is that he designed a new type of four-wheeled town carriage to be pulled by one horse, for ever more named after him: the brougham.

The chapel, which is still in use, is perhaps more interesting. Dedicated to St Wilfrid, it is reputed to be fourteenth century and was largely restored by Lady Anne Clifford in 1658. Lord

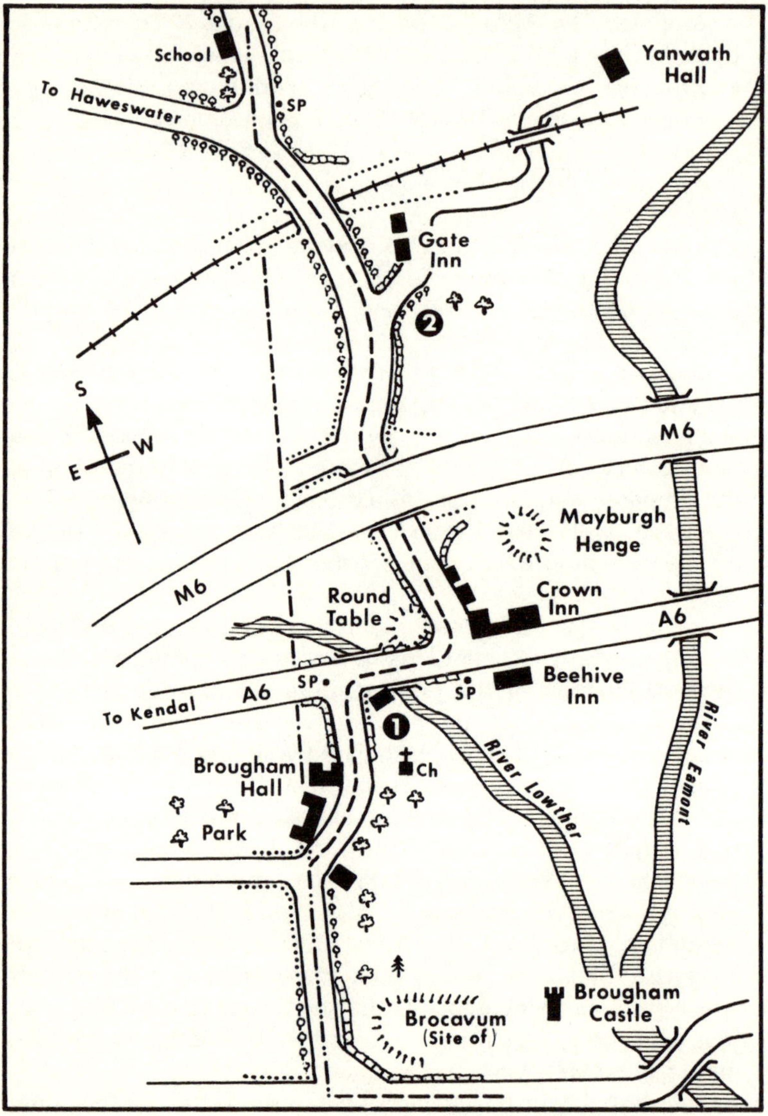
School
Yanwath Hall
To Haweswater
SP
Gate Inn
2
S
W
E
M6
Mayburgh Henge
Round Table
Crown Inn
A6
To Kendal
A6
SP
SP
Beehive Inn
1
Brougham Hall
Ch
River Lowther
River Eamont
Park
Brocavum (Site of)
Brougham Castle

Map 24

Brougham built the connecting bridgeway and other alterations to the chapel which have not received universal approval. It is still in use today.

A further half mile down the lane brings us to the A6 Kendal to Penrith highway. Turning right, we cross the River Lowther and enter the village of Eamont Bridge. The Lowther upstream borders the extensive grounds of the Lowther Estate, with its deer and wildlife parks and gardens. The Lowther caravan and camping site offers many facilities, including trout fishing. Lowther Castle is rather a sham, built in 1806 and now an empty shell, the grandiose frontage being all there is to see.

Eamont Bridge through the centuries has watched history flow past its doors. The Scottish raiders passed this way on their regular forays into England. 1715 saw the Jacobite rebels march through on the way to their defeat at the battle of Preston, and thirty years later the Young Pretender advanced and retreated along the same highway. Eamont Bridge was in those years a busy, bustling place with over thirty inns catering for the needs of travellers, packmen and drovers moving the vast herds of cattle to the great markets of Birmingham and London. The tax records of Carlisle in 1622 show that 18,574 head of cattle passed through the toll from the Galloway area on their way south. This trade attained its highest proportions about 1827 and was finally killed off with the advent of the railways.

The twentieth century brought another change as mechanized road transport developed and the new improved A6 carried a greatly increasing flow of heavy transport traffic over the notorious Shap Fell. The Shap Fell road now seems strangely quiet as the traffic thunders past along the M6 motorway on a new route along the lower slopes.

Eamont Bridge has not suffered quite the same fate as the deserted Shap – if suffered is the right word: it has the benefit of local traffic, and of course the tourist trade plays an increasing part in the economy of the region. It now has only two inns: the Crown Hotel, dated 1719, which provides food and excellent family accommodation, and across the road, the

Beehive Inn, a more modest establishment with a friendly atmosphere and bar snacks. The Beehive has an interesting history, being once kept by a Jacobite chaplain who turned innkeeper after the failure of the 1745 rebellion.

On entering Eamont Bridge, our way is by the first road on the left, indicated to lead to Ullswater and Tirril. The Bridge of Eamont lies further down the road towards Penrith; it was first built in 1291 but the present bridge was built by Bishop Langley in 1425 and is a fine example of a medieval bridge. It still retains its original narrow passway, the modern traffic being regulated by traffic signals.

As we turn left off the main road, evidence of early man's presence in the area can be seen. Known as King Arthur's Round Table, the henge is a grassy mound, five feet high and three hundred feet in diameter. Legend has it that Sir Lancelot fought here and defeated the Saxon giant Tarquin in single combat, and within the circle fifty champions battled for the hand of Arthur's daughter. It has been used over the centuries as a meeting place and the site of village fairs. Part of Charles II's Scottish army camped within it on their way south, but now it is still and empty, mainly ignored by the passing motorist. Access to the site is by a small wooden gate in the stone wall along our way, where a plaque, placed by Department of the Environment, informs the passer-by that the site dates from the Bronze Age, 1800 BC.

A further few hundred yards along our route we come to another, even older proof of the region's popularity with early man. Before crossing the M6 motorway, a small sliproad leads off to the right and is marked 'To the fish farm'. Look across the adjoining field and you will see what appears to be a small hill surmounted by trees. This is the Mayburgh Henge, a fifteen-foot-high, man-made arena convering $1\frac{1}{2}$ acres, the surrounding banks composed of river stones and pebbles from the nearby rivers. Within the arena stands an unhewn stone twelve feet high, the last survivor of an original eight. The purpose of the structure is unknown, but tales have been handed down of the Druids meeting here to perform their mystic rites, a sort of northern Stonehenge, and equally unlikely. There is a Victorian tale of the Romans using it to stage gladiatorial contests, and as the henge was built two thousand years before the Romans came to these islands, almost anything is possible. Its purpose today, though, is quite clear, as cattle graze within it. It can be entered through an opening on the north-east side.

Our route takes us across the motorway, and the road dips and turns through the lush pastureland. At about the two-mile mark, a narrower and older lane leads off to the right to reach the tiny village of Yanwath, which lies alongside the railway. The small, homely Gate Inn, adapted from an old tollhouse which gives it its name, provides bar snacks. I had hoped to find a Roman connection from its name through the Old English *Gatta*, meaning street or road, but the landlord was able to correct me. Further down the lane lies Yanworth Hall, a small memorial hall with a very fine square pele-tower, built in 1322 as a refuge against the Scottish border raiders; the tower is still in use as a store place for what is, and always has been, a working farm – a stark contrast to the grandiose ruins of the Victorian era not far away at Lowther.

Keen-eyes students of map-reading will notice an intriguing place-name on the Ordnance Survey maps about half way between the inn and Yanwath Hall: a building marked as 'The Grotto'. This is in fact a private house, and how it got its name and why it came to be so singled out as to be individually identified, I have been unable to discover. The only reference to it that I have been able to find is an account in the Westmorland Gazette of 1857 of a twenty-first birthday party, given by the then commanding officer of the Westmorland and Cumberland Yeomanry for his son, at his house near the foot of Ullswater. To quote: 'Mrs Hasell [the hostess] sat at the head of the first table and the five Misses Hasell and their sister Mrs Parker of The Grotto'.

Our curiosity unsatisfied, we continue across bridge spanning the main-line railway; a minor road leads off to the left, signposted to Haweswater and Askham, and our way is straight ahead.

Map 25

This next short section has been assumed to be along the original Roman alignment until we reach the village of Tirril. Near the junction with a side road, the alignment turns slightly more south to cross a series of cultivated fields to where, $1\frac{1}{2}$ miles on, we rejoin it at the farm drive of Winder Hall.

The small grey village boasts a Wesleyan chapel, a Quaker meeting house, a post office cum village shop and, of course, the Queen's Head Inn, dated 1719, which will, at the appropriate times, supply food and refreshments and, as already stated, could make an excellent base for the exploration of the area and a starting point for the next phase of the Roman route over High Street. For those wishing for more modest but equally pleasant accommodation, Winder Hall Farm, further still up the route, can provide bed and an excellent home-cooked breakfast. Pre-booking at both establishments would be advisable.

Leaving the Queen's Head, the route continues west towards Pooley Bridge. Judging by the number of notices advertising trout farms, it would appear that this is the new industry of the area, no doubt helped by the clear waters of the Eamont flowing nearby. Three-quarters of a mile along the road, a signpost indicates the way to Celleron and Haweswater; turn left up this very narrow, high-banked lane and begin the gradual climb out of the fertile valley to the moors ahead, as yet unseen. At the top of the lane, turn left at the junction, ignoring the footpath sign, and a few hundred yards will bring you to the gateway to the farm road leading to Winder Hall Farm. We are now on the true Roman alignment which has come direct across the fields from Tirril.

Map 26

At the end of the farm road, immediately beyond two farm cottages, the route bears right. Keep the dry-stone wall on your

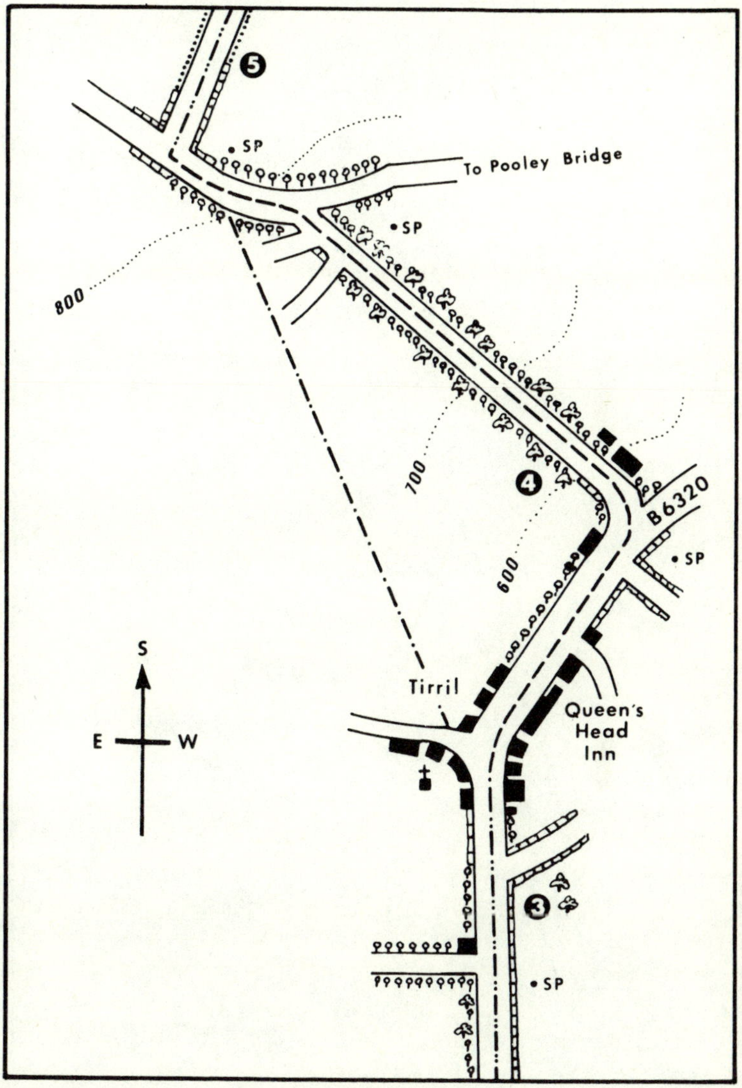

5
SP
To Pooley Bridge
SP
800
700
4
B6320
SP
600
S
E
W
Tirril
Queen's Head Inn
3
SP

Map 25

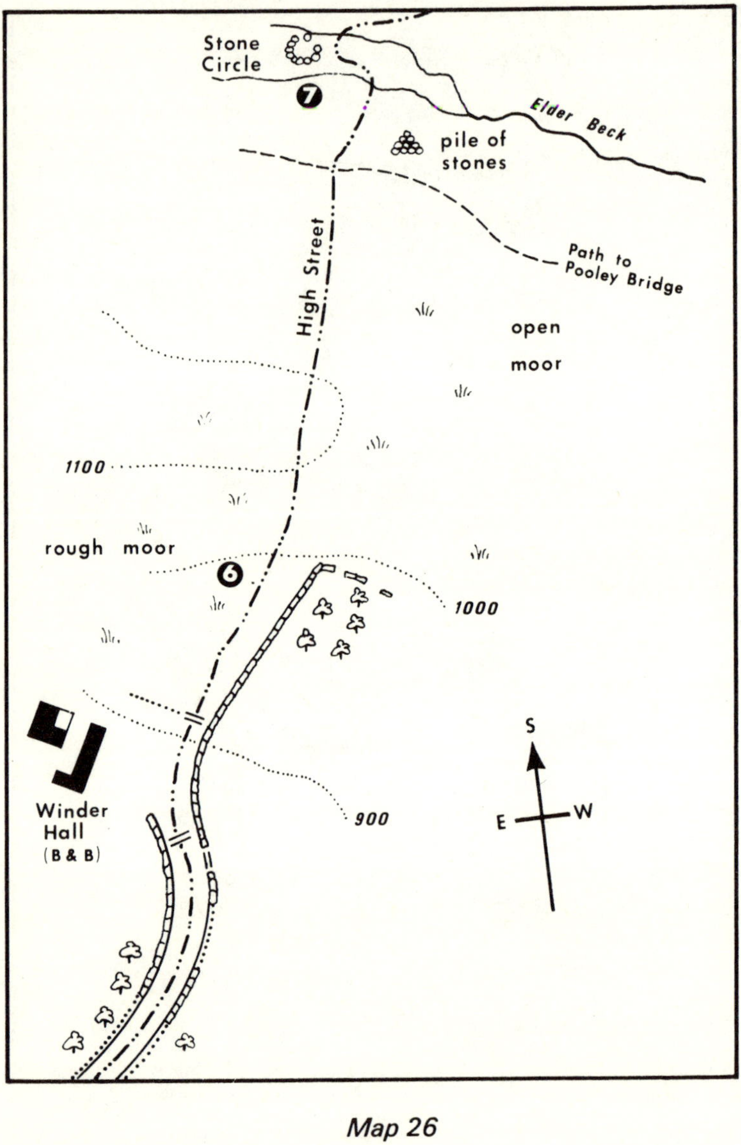
Stone Circle
7
Elder Beck
pile of stones
Path to Pooley Bridge
High Street
open moor
1100
rough moor
6
1000
S
E
W
Winder Hall (B & B)
900

Map 26

right to pass through a gate to reach the open fell. Winder Hall Farm, which is easily passed, hidden as it is by high walls, is a most attractive building. The manor farmhouse with its hidden courtyard and garden is a credit to the Carruther family who farm the property, and the date carved over the main entrance records that the present building was constructed in 1612.

The family have grazing rights on the open fellside, and the sheep are free to roam the fells during the summer months, to return to the lower ground in the late autumn. On the open fell the ground is for a while rough and the track indistinct; follow the line of the wall until it ends at a small plantation; bear slightly left along the contour of the fell to find a broad track heading south, and our first view of Ullswater comes into sight below. The track maintains its height along the slopes of Heughscar Hill before dropping steeply down to cross the trackway leading to the village of Pooley Bridge, which lies approximately two miles north-west at the northern tip of Ullswater. The bridge; from which the village gets its name, marks the old Westmorland and Cumberland boundary and is now very much a tourist spot, with hotels, guest houses and gift shops. Our way lies straight ahead, up the rising slope and crossing the small Elder Beck to reach an ancient stone circle.

The circle is one of a concentration of sites which abound in the area. Dated early and middle Bronze Age, they are to be found scattered along the fell sides, many located between five hundred and a thousand feet above sea level, which suggests a mild and drier climate of the period. The Roman route passes close to the circle, and it is strange that it managed to survive the road-builders, as the Romans were no respecters of native cults and practices.

Map 27

The true route turns slightly more west at this point and crosses the rough ground ahead on the eastern side of Aik Beck. There is no visible path, and the route at the best can only be seen as a faint line of ruts here and there; it is recommended only for the more experienced walker and not at all on a misty

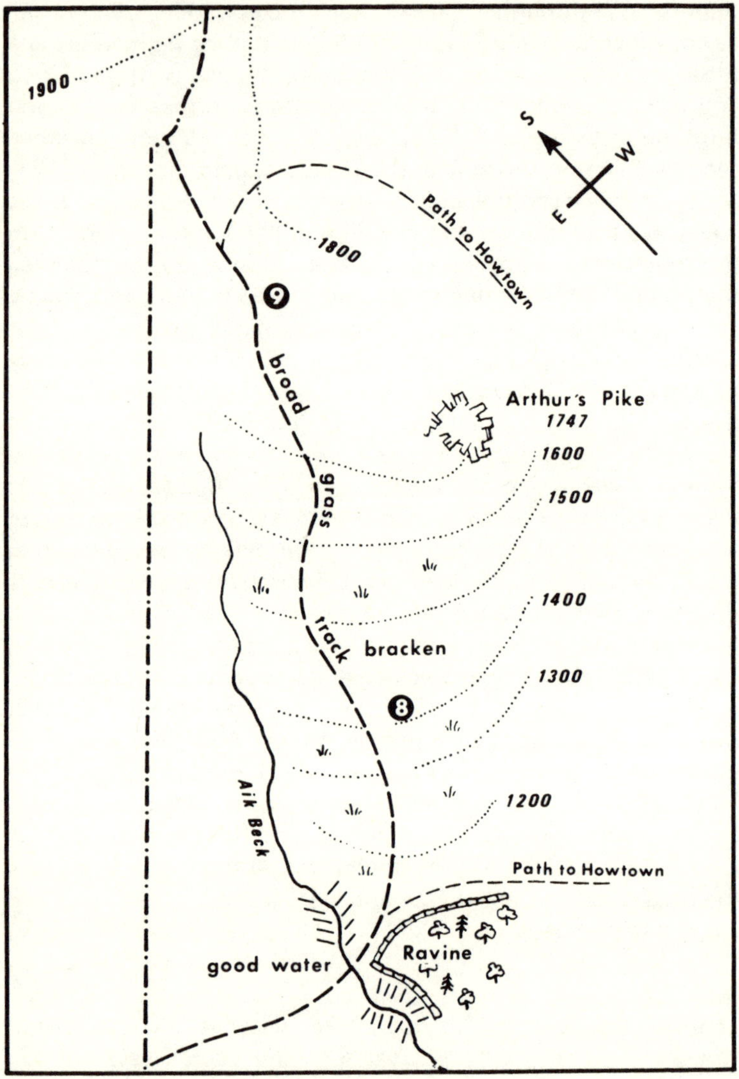
1900
S
W
E
Path to Howtown
1800
9
broad
Arthur's Pike
1747
1600
grass
1500
1400
track
bracken
1300
8
Aik Beck
1200
Path to Howtown
Ravine
good water

Map 27

day. A far better way is to make a diversion by turning right along the broad, easy-to-follow path, to the Aik Beck ravine. The path crosses the beck, but pause awhile to drink heartily of the pure, fresh water and replenish supplies, for this is the last fresh water obtainable for twelve miles. Do not be put off drinking the raw water on the high fells: it is like pure nectar compared to tap water; the story of finding a dead sheep in the stream higher up the fell has only happened to me once in years of taking the water, and even then I did not appear to suffer any harm.

Cross the beck and continue to follow the clear path to where it divides: one way leads down to Howtown, the other turns uphill to become a broad, grassy track between thick bracken and begins the long climb to our ultimate height of 2,700 feet.

As we climb and the magnificent scenery of the Lakeland hills begins to reveal itself, spare a thought for those early travellers, men of the legion who not only built the road but regularly tramped up and down it on their routine patrols. A 'century' of eighty heavily armed men, their semi-cylindrical shields in fitted goatskin covers slung over the left shoulder, short sword on the right side, dagger on the left. Each man carried two javelins as well as a pack containing his personal kit, rations, cooking utensils and combined trenching and turfing tool – all of which, together with plate armour and heavy iron and bronze helmet, must have weighed at least a hundred pounds. (See note 6.) Did they, I wonder, appreciate the view? Or would they be thinking of the sunny lands they had left behind and would most likely never see again? After his twenty-five years service the ex-legionary inevitably settled in the country in which he was serving at the time. There was no such thing as leave, and in the case of the Twentieth Legion, which arrived in force in AD 43, it remained on active service in Britain until the last cohorts marched away with Magnus Maximus in AD 383: 340 years of continuous active service.

There is an unlikely, but nevertheless interesting theory put forward by Arthur Weigall in his book *Wandering in Roman*

Britain. He correctly relates that in AD 383 a Spanish officer named Magnus Clemens Maximus, who held a high command in Britain, was proclaimed Emperor of the Western Empire by his troops in opposition to Gratian, who had succeeded Valentinian as Emperor. Maximus at once crossed to Gaul, taking with him some of the remaining units of the legions, including those of the Twentieth plus a large force of British auxiliaries. (See note 7.) He defeated Gratian near what is now known as the city of Paris and consequently rewarded his British troops by awarding them lands in Brittany. Mr Weigall's rather romantic theory is that this British blood came back to Britain seven hundred years later as followers of William the Conqueror, and so carried on, however remotely, the traditions and blood of the Romano-British legions seventeen generations later.

Between the eight- and nine-mile marks, the track skirts Arthur's Pike, a rocky outcrop on the right. A short detour is worth the effort to obtain a splendid view of Ullswater, twelve hundred feet below, and in the distance the high peaks of Skiddaw. After passing Arthur's Pike, the route levels and at the nine-mile mark the track, now only faint, divides, one part dropping down the fellside towards the tiny hamlet of Howtown where there is a mountain rescue post and what was once a small bobbin mill, a rural industry widespread throughout Westmorland in the mid-nineteenth century, depending on fast-flowing streams for water power and supplies of coppice wood.

Our way bears left to rejoin the true Roman route which has followed a course almost parallel to ours up the fellside. Although the route is not too clear at this point, it should not present any difficulties if you keep the rising ground of Loadpot Hill ahead and avoid losing height.

Map 28

The route soon becomes clear, and we now follow a well-defined and sometimes sunken track along the higher slopes of the approaching Loadpot Hill – this is marked on the

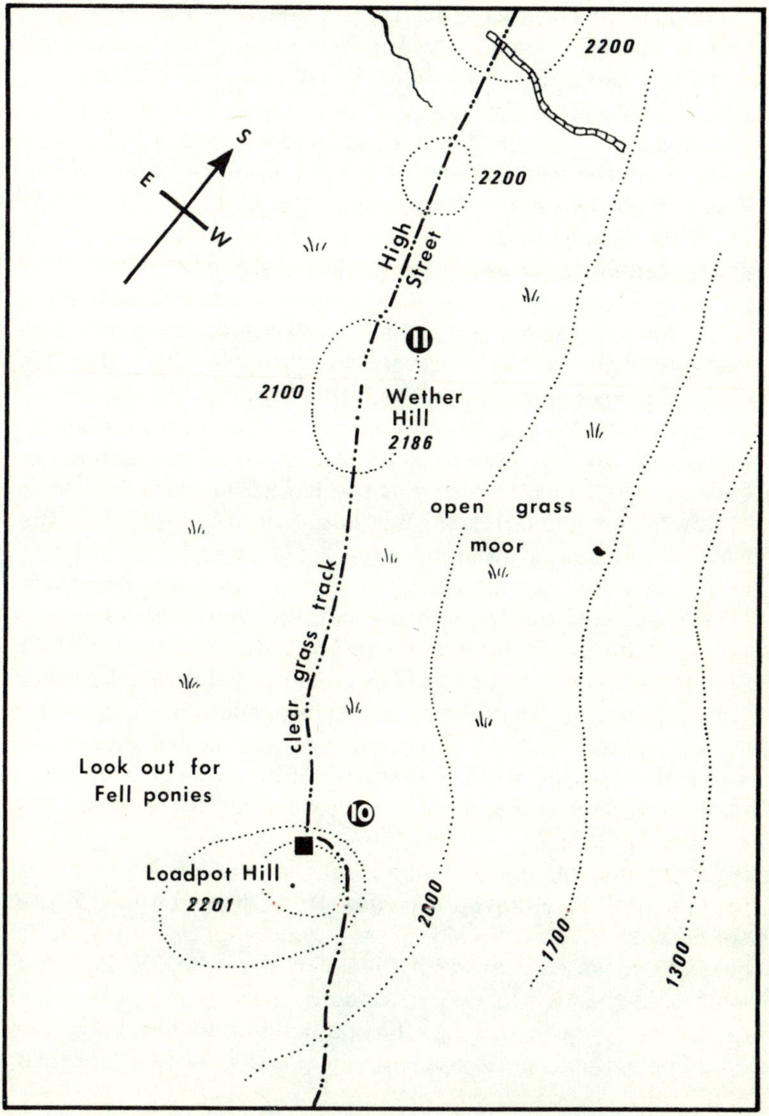
2200
S
E
W
2200
High Street
11
2100
Wether Hill
2186
open grass
moor
clear grass track
Look out for
Fell ponies
10
Loadpot Hill
2201
2000
1700
1300

Map 28

Ordnance Survey maps as 'High Street (course of Roman road)'. The immediate terrain is rather featureless and extremely desolate – you can almost hear the solitude, but wildlife abounds if you are lucky enough to spot it.

Apart from the inevitable sheep, the semi-wild fell ponies freely roam the hills and are often seen on these slopes, where they live all the year, going down to the farms to be fed only when the fells lie under deep snow. Groups of four or five will appear briefly on the skyline or round the shoulder of hill before galloping out of sight, their shaggy manes and tails streaming in the wind. These fell ponies have a direct link with our Roman past. A regiment of irregular cavalry called the Cunceus Frisiorium was stationed in the north towards the end of the occupation and was supplied with Frisian horses from Holland. Many fell owners recognize similar physical characteristics between their own ponies and the old Frisian breed.

The Martindale red deer often pass from their forest on The Nab further south, although they are a rarer sight. Birds of many varieties nest and feed in these high grasslands, safe from man; only the fox and the buzzard pose any threat.

The route skirts the summit of Loadpot to pass close to a unique landmark on this otherwise unremarkable hill: the stone chimney of Lowther House, a former shooting lodge and stables whose wooden structure was dismantled and taken away, to leave this solitary reminder of man's presence. It can make a welcome windbreak or shade from the sun on this treeless landscape.

The view of the Lakeland fells from Loadpot Hill is impressive, dominated by the Helvellyn range to the south-west. With the aid of Mr Wainwright's guide, it is possible to identify most of them. To the south is our next landmark, the twin grassy mounds of Wether Hill. The route can be clearly seen as it dips the odd hundred feet to rise gently on a fine, smooth grass track to a height of over two thousand feet.

Map 29

The next section of the route is good, easy walking, and the traveller can stride out in fine Roman style.

The two mounds which form the summit of Wether Hill are of a similar height separated by a shallow depression. The route traverses both of these as we head south, with, hopefully, the sun on our faces. The rugged, wild and indeed dramatic panorama of fells and mountains to the south and west makes up for the lack of features in the immediate surroundings. The smooth grassy track makes it possible to stride along and still appreciate the magnificent views without the worry of where we place our feet.

The route crosses the top of Keasgill Head, and a quarter of a mile further a dry-stone wall climbs the steep slope of Martindale Common to continue along the ridge. The track crosses through the wall to follow in the same direction along the edge of the ridge with a fine view of Martindale below. The cone-shaped hill due west is The Nab, with its famous deer reserve, which is completely out of bounds: in fact, there are no public footpaths at all in the dale, not that that would worry the true fell-wanderer over much. Along the way the route passes between the two small tarns of Redcrag, used as watering holes by both fell ponies and red deer.

The next section of the route is probably the most spectacular and more than justifies all the hard work so far. It covers the highest stretch of this, the highest Roman road in Britain, with the terrain falling away steeply on both sides of the narrow ridge. For this reason it would be foolhardy to continue beyond this point should a heavy mist descend; the only sensible course of action would be to retrace one's steps and return to the lower ground. I stated at the beginning of the chapter that there are no paths off the high fells; this is not strictly true, as those familiar with the area well know. These paths, of which there are several off Ramsgill Head, are in the main not very well defined and are difficult to follow in bad weather. It would be far safer to assume that my original statement stands and to stay with the main route.

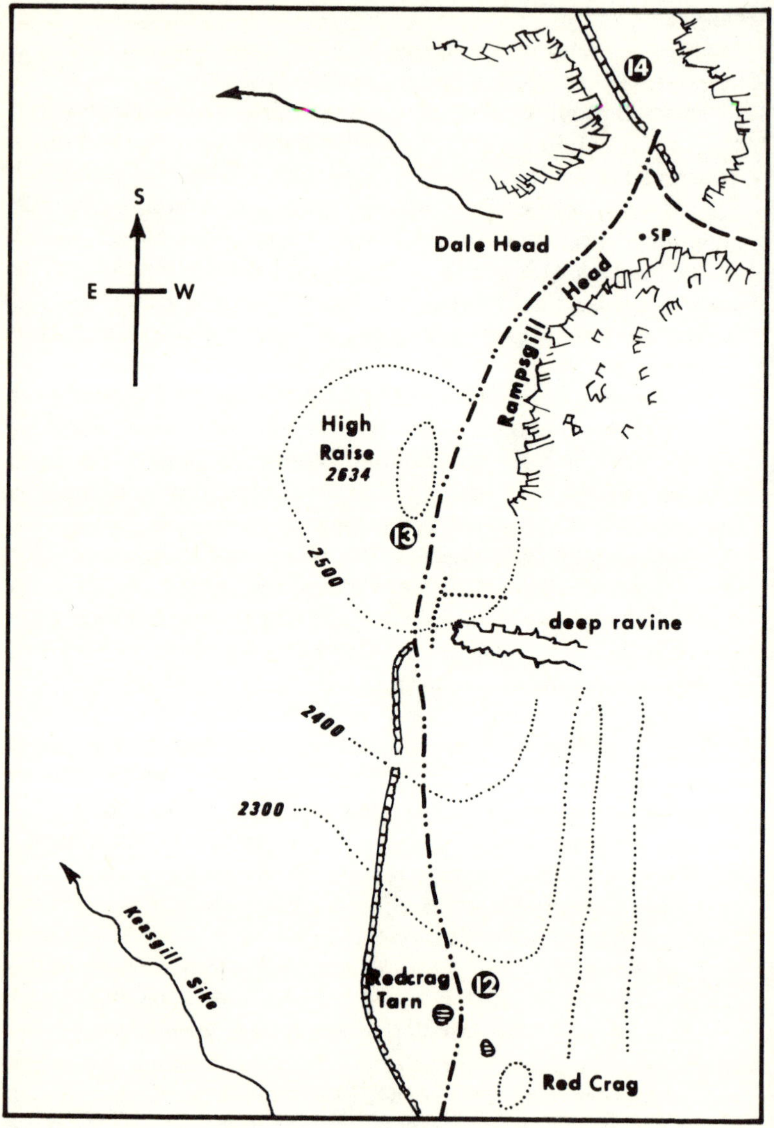
S
E
W
Dale Head
SP
Rampsgill Head
High Raise
2634
2500
deep ravine
2400
2300
Keasgill Sike
Redcrag Tarn
Red Crag
14
13
12

Map 29

Map 30

On the approach to the rising ground of High Raise at 2,634 feet, the route passes a sheer rocky ravine on the right protected by a wooden fence, and the dry-stone wall which as accompanied us on the left now ends. From the summit of High Raise the way ahead is clear along the grassy ridge, but it is the magnificent views in every direction which hold the attention. To the north and north-west we can retrace our route over Wether and Loadpot Hills with glimpses of Ullswater in the distance, to the east the Pennines and the Howgill Fells, and to the west the whole range of Lakeland peaks from Skiddaw to Coniston Old Man.

The track under foot is still good as the route turns westerly along the semi-circle of high ground enclosing the rough upper reaches of the valley of Ramsgill, with its steep slopes littered with boulder debris and scree. To the south the ground also drops sharply away down into Riggindale and to the shores of Haweswater. A guide post indicates the way and identifies the other routes already mentioned. Following the lie of the land, the route now turns due south, and we start along the long whalebacked crest of High Street.

High Street is one of the few mountain peaks to be mentioned in history. Until comparatively recently such high places were regarded as objects of awe and rarely visited, but not so High Street, which has been known and trodden through the centuries, by a mixed variety of travellers on an equally odd variety of missions. Bronze Age man probably used the route to avoid the dense, swampy valleys. The Romans, as we know, threw their road along it for the conquering legions. It was known in the thirteenth century as 'Brettestrete', the street of the Britons. The marauding Scottish raiders used it in their forays into the rich farmlands, and on one occasion were repulsed on the Troutbeck slopes. Later the local dalesmen and farmers made the summit their meeting-place for horse-racing and feasting, hauling hampers of food and ale up the two thousand feet from the dales below – on the large-scale maps the summit is still marked as Racehorse Hill. Nowadays all is

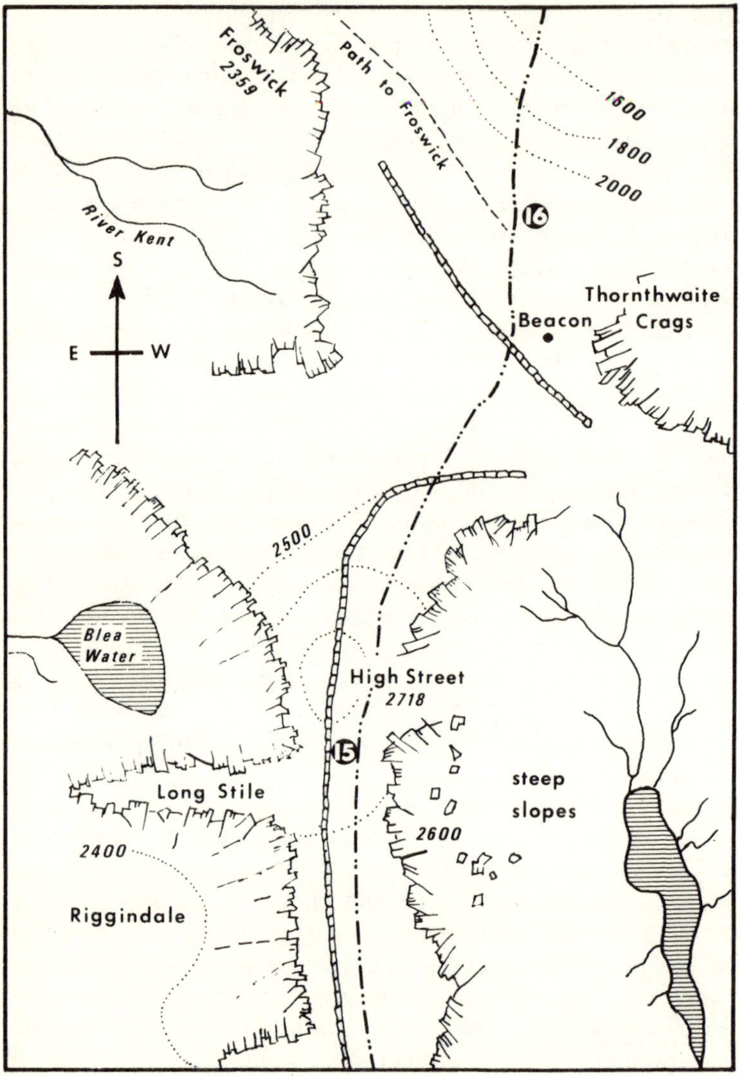
Froswick
2359
Path to Froswick
1600
1800
2000
16
River Kent
S
E
W
Thornthwaite
Beacon
Crags
2500
Blea
Water
High Street
2718
15
steep
slopes
Long Stile
2600
2400
Riggindale

Map 30

quiet, a grazing ground for sheep and sometimes the odd walker, for many consider it a dull place. How could such a pleasant place be dull, steeped as it is in the very bones of history?

Along the High Street ridge, the Roman road is the track to the west of the dry-stone wall, which is crossed soon after leaving Ramsgill Head, which incidentally is spelled 'Rampsgill' locally. Hayeswater, a small, quiet lake in a secluded valley, lies immediately to the west below the scree-covered slopes: Haweswater in Mardale stretches out to the east. Haweswater doubled in size when the dale was flooded to create a water supply for Manchester, and it is a lovely sight seen from the heights, although the shoreline can look ugly when the water level is low. The Ordnance Survey column which marks the summit lies on the other side of the wall, at 2,718 feet the highest point along the route. The well-marked track is easy to follow as it heads south along the edge of the ridge on a gently descending slope. There has been no evidence of a raised agger along any of the route so far; perhaps the Roman engineers felt that such a drainage system was unnecessary on the high-level ridges.

Map 31

As the track approaches the head of the valley of Hayeswater and a long ravine which marks the source of the gill, it passes through a stone wall before heading for a tall pillar of stones built on the rise slightly to the right: this marks Thornthwaite Crag. Its name derives from the long, shattered cliff facing west above the upper Troutbeck valley and marks the final stage of our journey. Cross the stone wall by the pillar for the first view of Troutbeck and the busy waters of Lake Windermere in two sections in the distance. From the pillar a faint narrow track leads downhill bearing to the left; a hundred yards further on the track divides: take the right-hand branch to drop diagonally and steeply down the fellside on a track marked as Scot Rake.

This is reputed to be the route taken by the Scottish raiders, although there are those who dispute such stories. Whether or

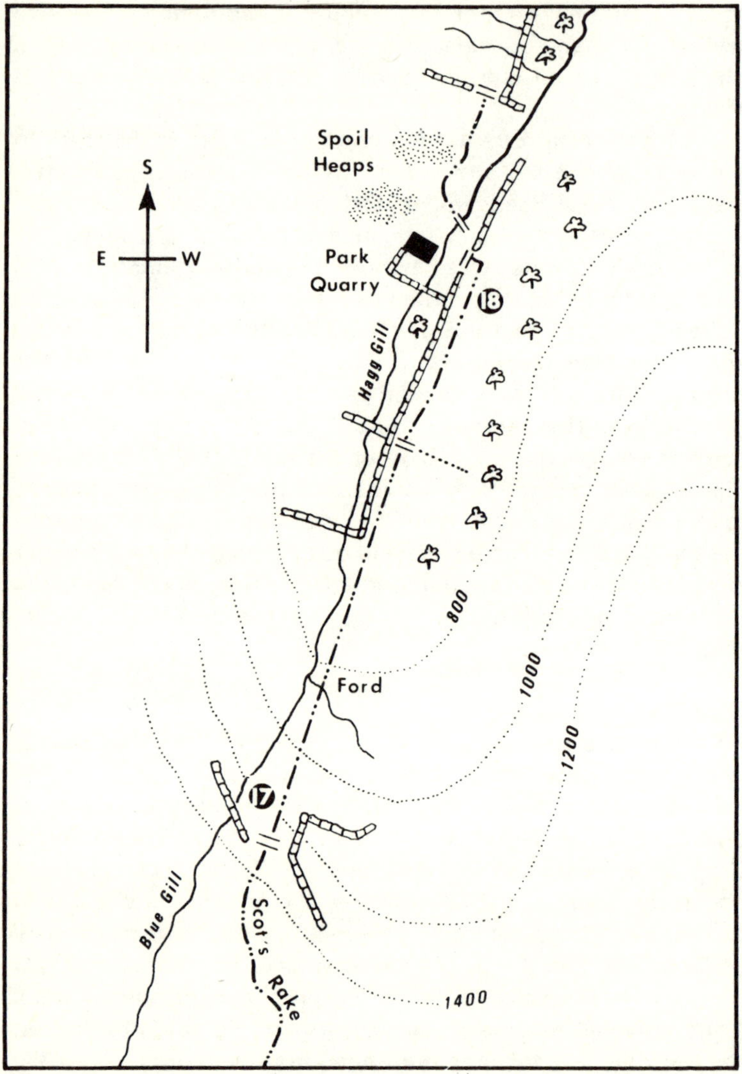
Spoil
Heaps
S
E
W
Park
Quarry
18
Hagg Gill
800
1000
Ford
1200
17
Blue Gill
Scot's
Rake
1400

Map 31

not the Scots came this way, I do not know, but the track is so narrow and steep that I find it difficult to believe that such a route was planned and constructed by the Roman legions. The point has been made by the experts that such a route would have been impossible for wheeled transport. This may not have worried the Romans over much as wide use was made of mules and packhorses, to which it would not have proved too difficult. The answer of course could be much more simple, in that the route up the side of Froswick could have been well terraced into the hillside on a zigzag path and that over the last nineteen hundred years it has suffered a landslide or series of landslides which have swept the original route away. Today the route drops a thousand feet in little over a mile, a weary descent, very hard on the legs. A good tip when descending a steep slope is to resist the natural tendency to lean backwards, but instead to lean forwards. This maintains your balance and a better grip underfoot.

As the severity of the descent eases, a stone wall comes in from the right and Hag Beck joins us on the left as it tumbles down from the heights of Froswick, a welcome sight for the thirsty traveller.

From this point the way is clear and easy to follow, passing through a gate and across a small ford. The stony farm track heads down the dale. The wooded slopes of The Tongue make a welcome change from the rather featureless terrain of the high peaks.

According to Margary, the Roman road now follows a route down the eastern side of the beck to the entrance to the valley and from thence to join up with the main Windermere to Ambleside road. There is a school of thought which suggests that the road would have been more likely to have taken a more western route from High Street via Caudale Moor and down Stock Gill to the fort at Ambleside. Although this later suggested route is certainly more direct, there is no evidence to support it, and in any case it would have been across very difficult and rocky terrain. It must also be remembered that the Roman road linking the fort at Watercrook, near Kendal, and

Ambleside, would most likely have followed the alignment now taken by the modern road, and the meeting of the two roads at the mouth of Troutbeck would have been logical. Further evidence to support this conclusion is a site now known as Low Borrans, situated to the west of the A592 high above the beck and approximately one mile from where the two roads could have met. The name 'Borrans' is quite common in the north-west, coming from the Norse word meaning 'a pile of stones' and is often associated with Roman remains. The fort of Ambleside, for instance, is sited in what is known as Borrans Field. It is possible that Low Borrans of Troutbeck could have been the site of some sort of staging post and stables for military couriers etc travelling to and fro along the High Street route.

Approximately one mile from joining the farm road, which now has a stone wall on our left, we approach Park Quarry (now disused). It is easily identified by its two spoil heaps and quarry building on the far side of the beck. Leave the road by a gate and cross the beck by the bridge to continue on a grass track past the spoil heaps of Lakeland slate. The slate industry of Troutbeck reached full production in 1753 with a great demand for roofing slates by the large expansion of the towns and cities of Britain. The slate was carried south and west to the coast by packhorses along well-established routes, and it is one of these routes, maybe adopted from the Roman route, that we follow now. Although the demand for slate has risen, it is doubtful that these small quarries will ever operate again., New roads would have to be built to carry the transport necessary, and thankfully that would prove to be uneconomic.

The bridlepath, for so it is designated, follows the contour of the fellside as it winds its way down the dale, not a typically accepted Roman route, you might think, but not so unusual where a level course was considered to be more important than a straight one. As we pass a heavily wooded area on the right, the path narrows, with high bracken on both sides, and numerous streams cross it, flowing down the steep slopes to the beck below. The rapid spread of bracken is cause of much concern in the Lakelands as it kills off the grass on which the sheep feed; only the fell ponies will eat it and to a small degree help by trampling it down. Spraying with herbicide has been tried with some success but proves expensive over a large area, although even this method comes under fire from the conservationists.

Leaving the trees behind, the path, now more open, continues with a dry-stone wall on the right and the steep slopes of the fellside above. The small river on the valley floor below is now the Trout Beck, having been joined by Hagg Beck as it flowed in from the western side of the Tongue. Looking back, the skyline is dominated by the high peaks we have just crossed, towering nearly two thousand feet above – an awesome sight for the traveller heading north, and although the guide can be used to cross the High Street in either direction, I think I would prefer the more gentle approach from the north ridge.

As we approach our first farmhouse since leaving Winder Hall, the route again crosses a series of streams, sometimes by bridge and sometimes by ford. In dry weather many are without water, but they soon fill rapidly if it rains on the peaks.

Map 32

After passing Long Green Head farm, our final destination comes into view and we leave the quiet and solitude of the hills as we approach the extensive Limefit Park caravan and camping site. The Roman route would probably have maintained its southern alignment, and there is indeed a track continuing in that direction. But for the sake of convenience I suggest that we break off the journey at this point and pass through the caravan park (There is a right of way) to the main entrance on the A592 Windermere to Patterdale road.

On reaching the main road, it is approximately three miles to the railway station at Windermere, where services connect with the main London to Scotland routes. During the summer months, the Mountain Goat Bus Company operates a fleet of minibuses around the Lakes which call at the entrance to the

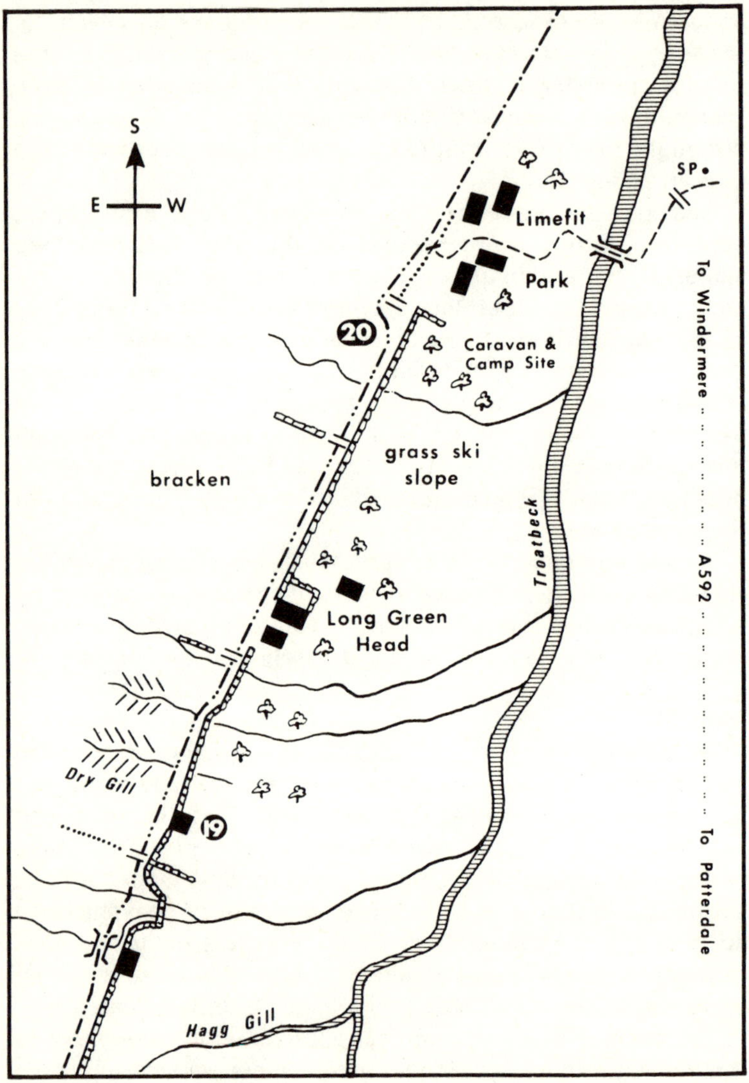
S
E
W
SP
Limefit
Park
20
Caravan &
Camp Site
grass ski
slope
bracken
Troutbeck
Long Green
Head
Dry Gill
19
Hagg Gill
To Windermere
A592
To Patterdale

Map 32

park on their way between Windermere and Ullswater several times a day.

The village of Troutbeck has no known Roman connections but nevertheless has much to interest the traveller. To reach the village, turn right up the main road and after about half a mile a narrow lane leads off to the left, soon to reach that part of the village known as High Green. Troutbeck is in fact a series of hamlets strung out for just over a mile along the fellside and dates roughly from the sixteenth century. At High Green the most notable feature is the Mortal Man Hotel and Inn, dated 1689, which boasts a sign bearing the following rhyme:

> O mortal man who lives by bread,
> What is it that makes your nose so red?
> Thou silly fool that looks so pale,
> 'Tis drinking Sally Birkett's Ale.

A feature of the village as you walk along its leafy lane and past its straggling clusters of cottages is the many springs or wells which feed the stone horse-troughs, placed there when the mail coaches travelled this way on their gruelling journey over the notorious Kirkstone Pass. These natural springs, which for centuries have supplied the local inhabitants, now bear a warning that the water is not fit for drinking. In honour of my namesake, your thirsty traveller drank deeply from St James's Well and, I am pleased to report, has suffered no harm. Incidentally, the Mortal Man Hotel offers food and rather up-market priced accommodation; much to the dismay of a hot and thirsty walker of Roman roads, it closes the public bar at 2.30 p.m.

Many of the cottages offer bed-and-breakfast accommodation, and others homemade scone-and-jam teas. Remarkably, the village has retained much of its old world charm unspoilt, despite its being so close to the tourist route over Kirkstone. At the south end of the village lies Town End, a fine example of a Lakeland yeoman's house, dated 1626. The farmhouse, lived in and farmed by the Browne family for four centuries until 1943, is now owned by the National Trust, who charge 90p entrance fee. William Hogarth, the satirist, hailed from Troutbeck, his father being a yeoman, i.e. small landowner, in the dale. Troutbeck church is situated on the lower road and contains a window designed by Sir Edward Burne-Jones, which shows a clean-shaven Christ on the cross. The church and school which lie nearby served not only the village but many of the outlying settlements and farms as far away as Kentmere and Longsleddale. A final peculiarity of Troutbeck is that, in spite of local government reorganization, it still has a mayor. The Mayor of Troutbeck has but two duties, one to start the annual hunt and later on the same day name his successor.

CHAPTER 5

Ambleside (Galava) to Ravenglass (Glannaventa) via the Roman fort at Hardknott Castle (Mediobogdum). Margary's route 740. 19 miles from Skelwith Bridge.

About the route

This road is, to a great degree, an extension of the previous route from the fort of Brocavum over High Street, connecting as it does the port and fort of Glannaventa at Ravenglass and so opening up an important supply route for the northern province. The Roman navy, named in Britain the *Classis Britannica*, had its headquarters at Boulogne. It was from time to time used in offensive warfare, but its main and more enduring role was that of transport and the supply of the military forces, and as such it was to play an important part in the defence and control of northern Britain. The fort at Ravenglass is thought to have been built in the reign of the Emperor Hadrian, 117–38, so we may assume that the connecting road was constructed somewhere around that period.

The first two miles of the route from the fort site at Ambleside I have omitted, for this has been mainly adopted by the present road which follows the course of the River Brathay along the edge of the valley slightly raised above the river level. The name 'Brathay' comes from Old Norse meaning 'broad river', which apparently was prone to flooding in former days so that the course taken by the road is the only possible one. Unfortunately this road is rather busy in the summer months and is for the most part without a pedestrian way; I therefore suggest that one starts the walk at Skelwith Bridge.

The route divides well into three sections. The first is a delightful, easy walk through woodlands and on well-defined footpaths and tracks along the south side of Little Langdale, with magnificent views of the Langdale Pikes to the north. The second section includes the long, steady climb up and over Wrynose Pass and the easier climb by the Roman route up Hardknott at 1,240 feet, to gaze down on the high walls and headquarters block of the Roman fort of Mediobogdum on the spur of land five hundred feet below, dominating the Esk valley. The third and final section is equally enjoyable, a fine packhorse route well off the beaten track, through quiet woodlands and pastures down the side of the valley of the Esk to the fort site on the coast and the Roman bath house.

Spring, summer or autumn would be the best times to attempt the route, although I am sure that there are occasions when a winter excursion would be most invigorating, for the winter scenery must be magnificent. The centre section, from the bottom of Wrynose Pass to the Woolpack Inn in Eskdale, is the wildest and most remote, with practically no shelter should the elements prove inhospitable, and I certainly would not attempt it if heavy rain threatened. Accommodation is plentiful at all levels in Ambleside, whilst in Little Langdale it is limited to the Three Shires Inn and one or two bed-and-breakfast farmhouses. Eskdale has a limited selection, including the Woolpack Inn just off the route and several farmhouses mentioned in the text. Ravenglass again has limited accommodation, details of which can be obtained from the Information Bureau near the railway station.

No special equipment is required, although good waterproofs would be prudent as the weather can change rapidly in the hills. Do not be tempted by the sun to dress too lightly, as the winds can be very cold where the route traverses the high, exposed passes. Otherwise, with a stout pair of boots or walking shoes, a fine walk lies ahead.

As on other routes, as well as the guide an Ordnance Survey

map of the area is recommended to give the wider view. In this case an excellent choice would be the Outdoor Leisure Range, $2\frac{1}{2}$ inches to one mile, *The English Lakes*, south-west sheet, which includes most of the route. To cover the first part of the route, use the south-east sheet, although the smaller-scale map of Ambleside would suffice. I would also recommend *The Pictorial Guide to the Lakeland Fells* by A. Wainwright, Book 4.

The Route
Map 33

The site of the Roman fort of Galava at Ambleside (map ref. NY3703) lies in Borrans Field on the south side of a link road between the A593 and A591, bypassing the centre of the town. The site has been excavated on several occasions, and two gates, some angle towers and the central range of buildings of the stone fort have been revealed. The site is owned by the National Trust, who have provided a plan to identify the various structures; the tops of the walls have been turfed, which leaves a rather overgrown impression of the site. The visible stone fort was built in the second century and continued in use to well into the fourth. An earlier fort, on a slightly different site, was built of turf and timber and was thought at one time to date from the Agricolan period. This has since been discounted, and the earliest date for this site has now been confirmed at AD 90.

There are no surviving records to tell us of the garrison of the fort. The discovery of a paved parade ground outside the fort indicates that it was garrisoned by a unit of infantry. One inscription tells us that a records clerk by the name of Flavius Rommus, aged thirty-five years, was killed within the fort – we assume from enemy action, which in itself would be a most unusual thing to have happened. There was, though, a successful concerted attack on the northern province in 367–8, a disaster made the greater by a serious breakdown of discipline in the Roman army and general disorder. It took two years for the government to regain control.

The finds from the site can be seen at the National Parks

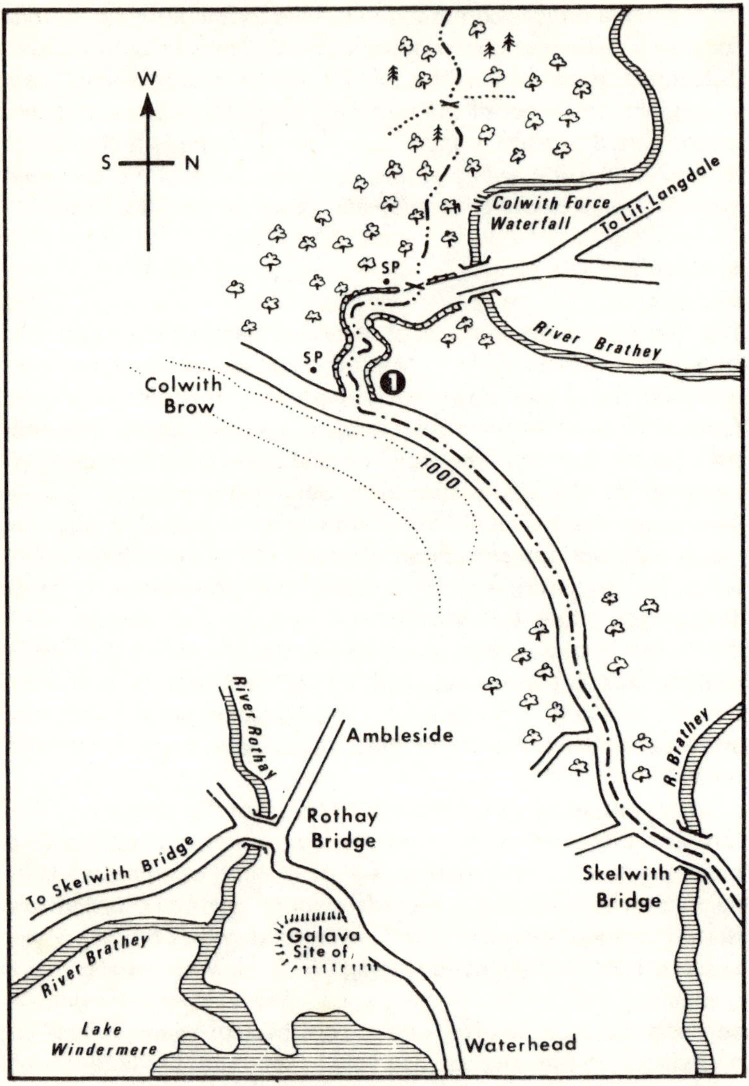
W
S
N
Colwith Force
Waterfall
To Lit. Langdale
SP
SP
River Brathey
Colwith
Brow
1000
River Rothay
Ambleside
R. Brathey
Rothay
Bridge
To Skelwith Bridge
Skelwith
Bridge
Galava
Site of
River Brathey
Lake
Windermere
Waterhead

Map 33

Centre at Brockhole, two miles south on the Windermere road, although some of the information is a little out of date and needs revising.

From Skelwith Bridge take the road marked to Coniston. This climbs steadily up and around the lower slopes of Park Fell, with Great Langdale stretching out to the north. After approximately one mile we reach a minor road, signposted to Little Langdale. The narrow road drops down the fellside in a zigzag, and it is here that Margary claims that traces of the original Roman route can be detected on a similar course, but unfortunately the ground is much overgrown, and any possible traces are hidden. The lane, between dry-stone walls, reaches the valley bottom and crosses the River Brathay. Our way is to cross by two stiles into the wood on the left of the lane just before the bridge is reached. A signpost indicates the footpath to High Park. The woodland path climbs a small hill as it meanders between the trees, the river not far below, within hearing if not in sight. The ground drops again and the path closes on the river as it approaches the twin falls of Colwith Force where the river bed drops over a small cliff into a deep basin below. Continuing along the path, we leave the course of the river and cross over a stile into a fenced plantation of mixed trees. Several small streams cross the route as it gently climbs out of the wood through a gate into an open pasture.

Map 34

Immediately ahead is the craggy top of Great How. Keeping the wall on your right, a gateway leads to a path through a small field and a gate by High Park Farm. Leave the farmyard across the cattle-grid into the walled lane. (Bed-and-breakfast accommodation is available here.)

We are now on the true route, along a westerly alignment which is generally maintained until we reach the valley bottom at Bridge End. The route follows a level contour for much of the way as it keeps to the lower slopes on the south side of the dale. The track here is tarmacked and terraced into the steep slope of the fellside, with rich pastureland down to the river

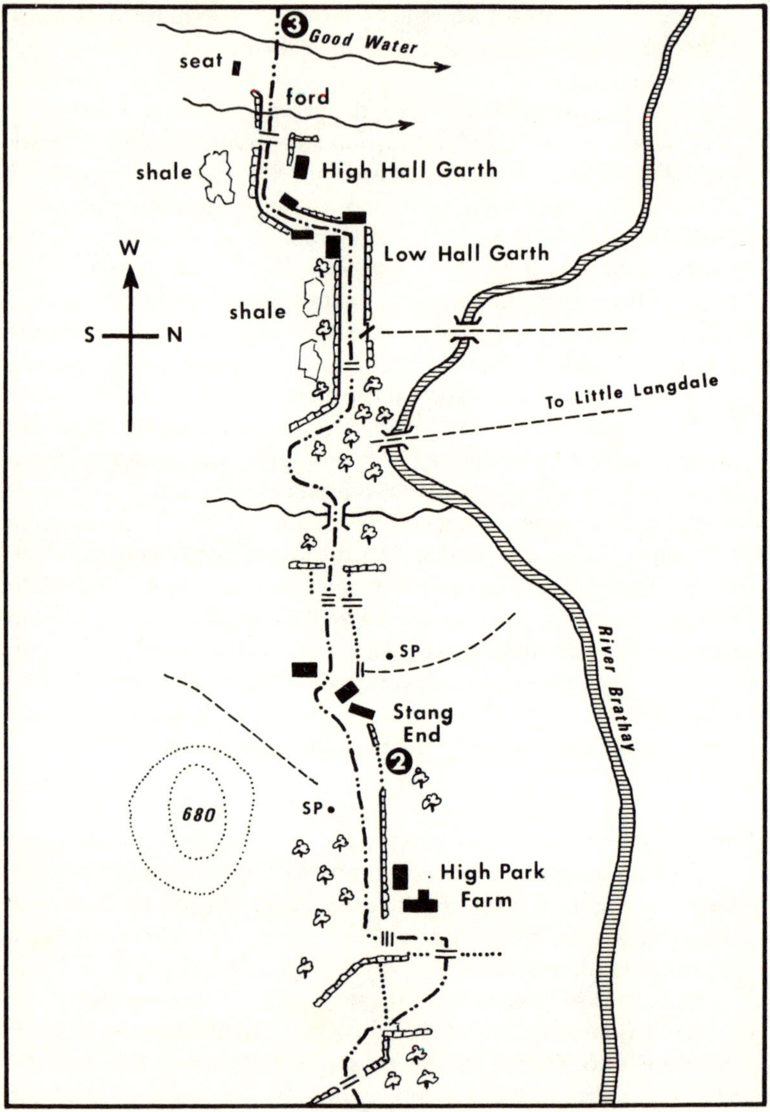
3
Good Water
seat
ford
shale
High Hall Garth
Low Hall Garth
W
S
N
shale
To Little Langdale
SP
Stang
End
2
River Brathay
680
SP
High Park
Farm

Map 34

below. Small herds of Cumbrian cattle and scattered Lakeland sheep are the only signs of life under the hot sun of a July day. A footpath sign indicates the way to Hodge Close as we approach Stang End Farm. At the farm (its name derived from the Old Norse meaning 'boundary stone') our way is between the two farm buildings downhill onto a well-made track. A sign on the right indicates the way to Little Langdale across the river.

Following the same alignment, the track drops slightly and after a cattle-grid crosses a small stream to enter the edge of a wood. The track makes a slight detour to avoid a small hill before returning to its alignment, this time with the river alongside. Here a ford and well-made bridge cross the river with a path to the village and the Three Shires Inn, half a mile away. As previously stated, the inn provides accommodation, a restaurant in the evening, and bar snacks at lunchtime, including fresh salmon and venison.

As the river wanders off to the north, we pass high heaps of shale behind the stone wall on our left, spoil heaps from the disused quarry further up the hillside, whilst on our right the lush river meadow rich with buttercups is bordered by the pink blossoms of wild roses.

As we round the shoulder of the fell, our first view of Wrynose Pass comes into sight, with tiny cars crawling slowly to the top. A stile in the wall on the right points the way to a small hump-backed bridge, another footpath crossing of the river and called Slater Bridge. This unusual bridge is constructed of large slabs of slate and is believed to have been built by quarrymen from the great slate quarries of Tilberthwaite and Hodge Close.

The route, now between dry-stone walls, passes a farm building, marked on the map as a climbing hut, owned by the National Trust and named Low Hall Garth. The track now becomes very rough and stony as it turns uphill for a short distance, passing a further spoil heap of slate before passing High Hall Garth and out of the enclosed lane onto the open fell. The still rough track now begins a gentle descent of the fell, and two streams cross the route; the second one, coming down from Knott Head, provides good, clear drinking water as it splashes over a small waterfall. On a wooden seat just above the route and in commemoration of 'E.M. 1945–75', I sat awhile in memory of this unknown person's thirty years of obvious pleasure, and a well-earned rest. Below, Little Langdale Tarn lies smooth and tranquil, and a mixed herd of cattle laze in the lush meadow around its shore.

The route is now approaching the head of the dale, the high peaks presenting a huge U-shaped, seemingly impossible barrier to any further progress to the west and our ultimate destination, the sea. One cannot help but admire the tenacity of the Roman engineers who pioneered this (even with modern transport) rigorous and demanding route over the high pass of Wrynose.

Map 35

The track continues to descend until the dale bottom is reached near Bridge End Farm. The true Roman route has been lost as it crosses the low-lying land, and there is no trace until it reappears, according to Margary, at Pedder's Stone on the road over the pass. Our route is to continue along the enclosed lane which crosses the river meadow between the two streams, the tall grasses speckled with the colour of wild flowers and the orange and brown butterflies feeding upon them. Crossing the now infant Brathay by the footbridge we join the main (for the most part single-track) road, to start our ascent of Wrynose.

On the way we pass the aptly named Fell Foot Farm with its unusual rounded chimneys. Go through the gate across the road (which we are requested to keep closed) and begin the slow climb. There is one consolation along this section: what traffic there is, and there is a fair quantity at weekends in the summer, doesn't move very much faster than the walker as it negotiates the narrow, tight bends and steep gradients. As the road passes the small crag on the right called Castle Howe, the rough fell falls away to the north into a tiny dale and Blea Tarn, unseen from the road. The ground on the left obscures for a

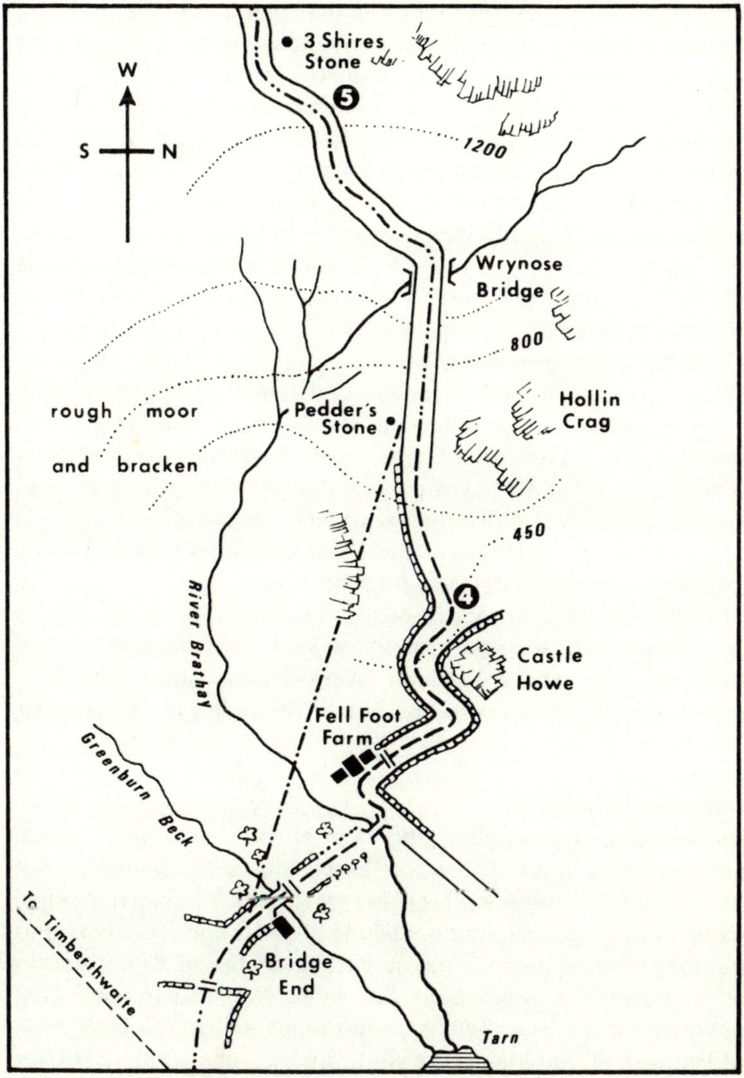
3 Shires
Stone
W
S
N
1200
Wrynose
Bridge
800
Hollin
Crag
rough moor
and bracken
Pedder's
Stone
450
River Brathay
Castle
Howe
Fell Foot
Farm
Greenburn Beck
To Timberthwaite
Bridge
End
Tarn

Map 35

time the view to the south, but as the road continues to rise, it passes under the rocky crags of Wrynose Fell with the ground now falling steeply down into the dale head below, the bracken-covered slopes relieved by the swaying heads of hollyhocks. A native plant, the hollyhock was cultivated in Romano-British times, with herbs such as parsley, fennel and coriander for their pot and medicinal properties.

As previously mentioned, according to Margary, traces of the Roman road can be seen near Pedder's Stone, and therein lies a difficulty as I was not able to identify which *was* Pedder's Stone, as there are so many stones along the route. I *was* able to detect a possible section of the original route just below Wrynose Bridge to the north of the present road, where a terraced section is cut into the hillside, although the fell is so overgrown with bracken that it is difficult to be certain. I think the important thing is that we are following the general line of the Roman route and should not be over-concerned with technicalities.

Pause awhile at Wrynose Bridge: the water is cool and clear, and the views of the dale are breathtaking.

Climbing once more, our next landmark is the Three Shires Stone marking the old boundary and the meeting of the three counties of Cumberland, Westmorland and Lancashire, before the reorganization. The Three Shires Inn is named after this stone.

Map 36

As the summit is reached, the view ahead opens up to reveal another of the many fine sights along this route. Stretched out below is an almost perfect example of a U-shaped valley, carved out by glacier action millions of years ago. The rock- and boulder-covered slopes drop steeply down to the River Duddon as it snakes its way down the valley bed towards its final destination, the Irish Sea, fourteen miles away. The high peak of Harter Fell dominates the route as it climbs tortuously over Hardknott Pass on the far horizon.

As we pause for breath, we can imagine the Roman surveyors setting up their sighting apparatus and lining it up

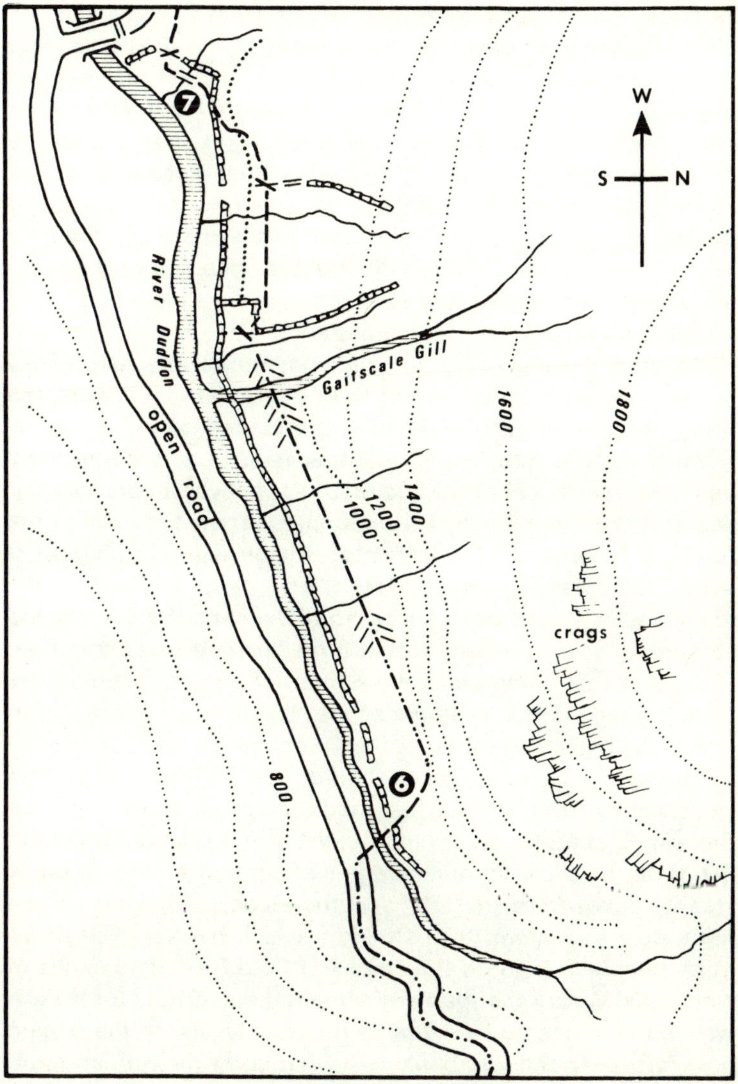
W
S
N
River Duddon
Gaitscale Gill
open road
1600
1800
1400
1200
1000
800
crags
7
6

Map 36

with the smoke signal from their advance party. This would be directly across the valley on the summit of the next pass over the mountain range to the west; both passes are at the same height of 1,240 feet. The alignment fixed, the engineers would then direct the building of the road itself, taking a zigzag course down the steep gradient until the valley floor was reached. The chosen alignment would then be followed, in this case along the flat ground on the north side of the valley between the river and the steep slopes. In hot, dry weather, the line of the route can sometimes be detected from the top of the pass as a broad scorchmark across the rough grassland.

What of the men who actually constructed the road? They left no records but it is more than likely that they were the same men who also built and garrisoned the fort below Hardknott Pass, and these we know belonged to an auxiliary unit, the fourth cohort of Dalmatians, a five-hundred-strong cohort who had originally been recruited on the far coast of the Adriatic, in what is now known as Yugoslavia. They had first come to Britain in AD 43 or AD 61, and although early replacement would have come from Dalmatia, by the second century local recruitment would have become quite common. They would be commanded by Roman officers and could have been working in this case under the directions of experts from one of the legions, most likely the Twentieth Legion.

The modern single-tracked road adopts the Roman route as it descends, and cannot be much of an improvement, as thousands of motorists will agree; the 1 in 4 gradient and tight bends do not allow for much degree of error. The ground comes steeply down from the left, and the slope continuing on the right, down to infant River Duddon, which has tumbled down from its source high on the slopes of Cold Pike, by a series of waterfalls. Where the road and stream meet, it runs for a short way within a deep ravine, but as the road levels, so the stream now runs between low banks. At what point the Roman route leaves the metalled road I was unable to ascertain; according to Margary, it crosses several times before reaching Wrynose Bottom, where it can be more easily detected.

I suggest that the walker, on reaching level ground, cross the stream at the first possible opportunity, cross through the ruined dry-stone walls which runs alongside the stream for much of its way, and take a route over the rough grassland along sheeptracks on the lower slopes, thus avoiding the boggy, flat land. Very soon the valley bottom widens as we clear Wrynose Breast with its scree-covered slopes (no shortage of road-building materials here), and the route becomes more easily detected as a raised agger on the flat ledge of ground several feet above the valley bed.

Here the walking is good along a grass track; the silence can be almost heard; the odd car passes quietly along the open road close to and south of the winding stream, the young River Duddon. Far ahead on the slopes of Hardknott the occasional flash of sunlight reveals the presence of other travellers making their tortuous way by car up the 1 in 3 gradient. As the route approaches Gaitscale Gill, the agger becomes pronounced as a causeway and can clearly be seen on either side of the wide, rocky gill.

On both occasions when I crossed the gill, there had not been any water coming down off the high fell and I experienced no difficulty, but if after heavy rain the gill becomes a raging torrent, on no account attempt a crossing. As can be seen when it is dry, although some parts are quite shallow, there are also very deep pools to trap the unwary. Should this situation occur, abandon the Roman route at this point and make the easier crossing of the Duddon upstream of the gill, proceeding by the metalled road to Cockley Beck Bridge.

On successfully crossing the gill, continue along the causeway towards a dry-stone wall across the route. Where the wall ends and a fence takes over, a stile (broken at the time of my last passing) gives access to a small enclosure; pass through the ruined wall to regain the alignment along a broad, grassy, well-defined track. The track follows close to the stream as it takes a wide bend to the north, momentarily leaving the roadway, and a wire fence now keeps us company on our left. After crossing a small stream, another dry-stone wall bars the way, crossed by yet another broken stile near the wire fence and a further stream is crossed; look out for a slight gap (the top wire is missing) in the wire fence; cross this to pass between the fence now on your right and a dry-stone wall. Follow the wall until a gap occurs to reveal a stone foot-bridge across Moasdale Beck immediately north of its junction with the Dunnon by Cockley Beck Bridge. On crossing the beck, a few steps take you to a stile over the wall on your right and access to the metalled road now beginning its climb to Hardknott Pass.

Map 37

Our way, and the true Roman route, is across the road to a farm track heading south-west, passing shortly through a gate onto the private road to Black Hall Farm, now converted into a youth hostel.

This narrow, stony track is laid upon an agger twenty feet wide and slightly raised above the natural ground level, and although the track follows a gently winding course, the Roman agger heads straight for the wooded slopes of Harter Fell. These lower slopes form part of the Forestry Commission's Dunnerdale Forest. Looming high above the forest is the rocky summit at the height of 1,620 feet.

The true route, after crossing Hardknott Hill, passes to the east of the farm at the end of the track and swings south before doubling back to the north-west in a sweeping curve east of a ruined sheepfold. Our way is through the yard of Black Hall Farm, passing between the two main buidings and running the gauntlet of numerous barking dogs, to a gate which gives access to a field pasture. Follow the right-hand wall to a further gate onto the open fell. The Roman route can here be detected as a broad green track as it curves up the fellside to pass by the previously mentioned ruined sheepfold and then climbs up in a series of zigzags. Due to the rough nature of the ground, plus the ravages of time, it is not easy or practical to follow the precise route for all the way up the fell. In case of difficulty, head diagonally up and across towards the boundary fence of

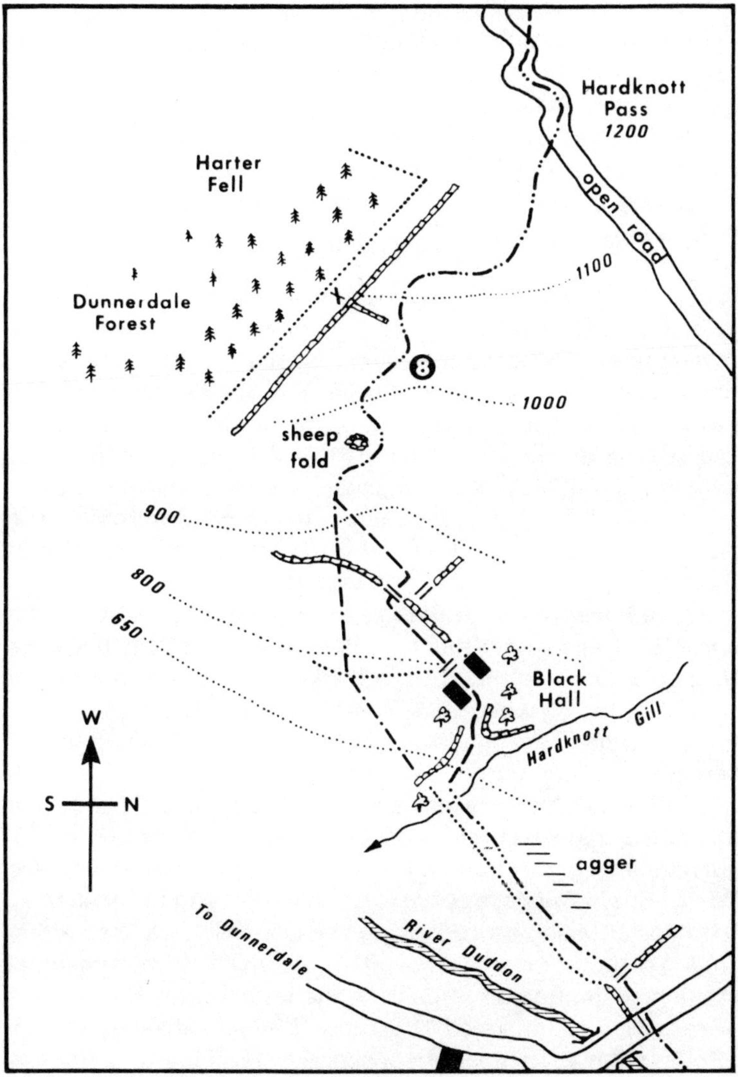
Hardknott
Pass
1200
Harter
Fell
open road
1100
Dunnerdale
Forest
8
1000
sheep
fold
900
800
650
Black
Hall
W
S
N
Hardknott Gill
agger
To Dunnerdale
River Duddon

Map 37

the plantation; here a rough grassy and sometimes boggy path continues uphill between the fence and a broken dry-stone wall, until the summit is reached and it meets the metalled road on Hardknott Pass at 1,240 feet.

The route as described from the bottom of Wrynose Pass to the summit of Hardknott Pass is in the main along a public footpath and lies within the National Park Access Area.

Map 38

Continue along the metalled road for two hundred yards before swinging north to pass through a rocky spur of Raven Crag in a cutting fifteen feet deep and where the road is fifteen feet wide, running north of the present road in the direction of the fort to be plainly seen five hundred feet below the summit of the pass. Our way is by the public footpath which swings north-west around the artificially levelled parade-ground about three acres in size with its raised tribunal or inspection dais. The parade-ground lies two hundred yards east of the east gate of the fort.

As you descend from the head of the pass, the view to the north-west and north must be one of the finest in the Lake District, as tier upon tier of crags and peaks stretch out before us, whilst to the west there is the sea and, on a clear day or towards sunset, the shadowy form of the Isle of Man on the far horizon.

The Roman fort of Mediobogdum, (Grid Ref. NY2101) 'the fort in the middle of the bend' on the River Esk, is one of the outstanding sites of Roman Britain. It is also the best-preserved Roman fort in Britain, outside Hadrian's Wall, and because of its spectacular position overlooking the Esk valley and its setting amongst these magnificent fells it is, in my view, the most exciting of the Roman remains in the British Isles. Excavations were carried out between 1890 and 1894 and again during the 1960s, when a fragmentary inscription revealed that the fort was built in the reign of Hadrian and garrisoned by the fourth cohort of Dalmatians, as mentioned earlier in the chapter. It was evacuated around AD 140, when the frontier was moved

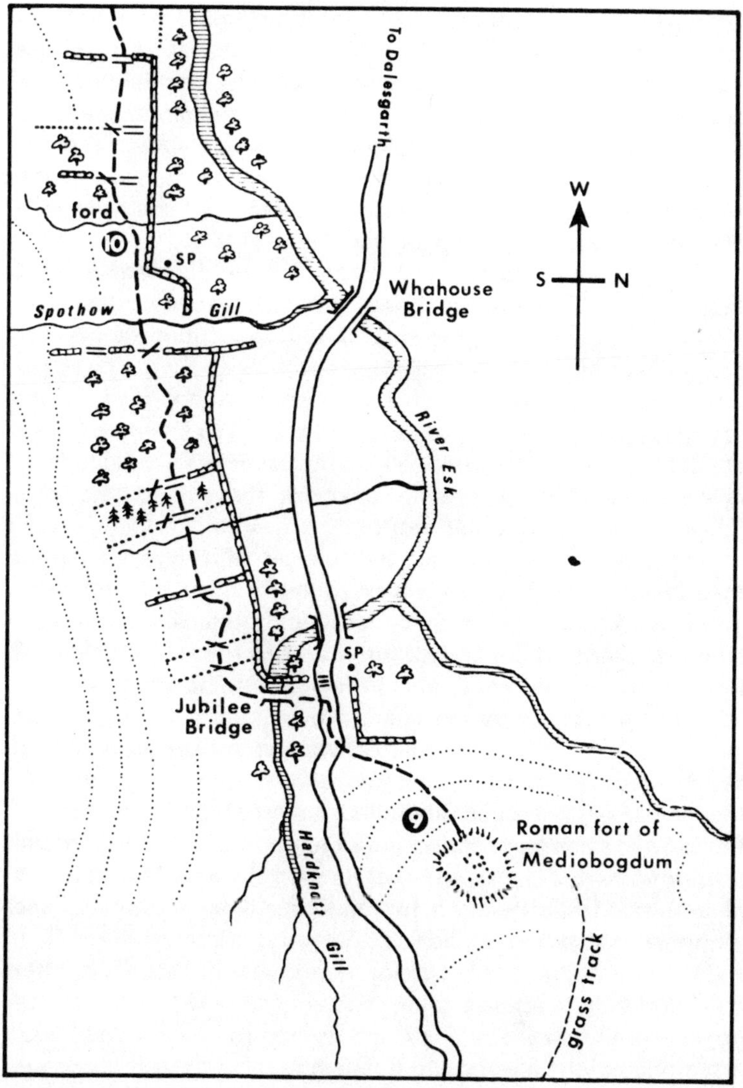
To Dalesgarth
W
S
N
ford
10
SP
Whahouse
Bridge
Spothow
Gill
River Esk
SP
Jubilee
Bridge
9
Roman fort of
Mediobogdum
Hardknott
Gill
grass track

Map 38

northwards into Scotland, but was reoccupied and partially rebuilt under Governor Agricola Calpurnius in AD 163. It does not, however, appear to have been in use beyond the end of the second century. It probably owes its excellent state of preservation to its isolated position, for it would appear that the greatest enemy of these early builders was not necessarily the elements but man himself, who plundered the sites for handy building material, right up to the Victorian Era.

Unlike so many ancient sites, you will be pleased to know that there is no admittance fee; that has already been paid, along the hair-raising gradients. A full description of the site can be found in *A Guide to Roman Remains in Britain* by Roger J.A. Wilson, and it is not for me to repeat his work. Sufficient to say that the entire circuit of fort walls stands to a superb height of eight to ten feet, although some have been rebuilt from fallen stone. A slate course separates the original standing masonry from the rebuilt work.

The main Roman road passed the fort thirty yards north of the present road. After inspection of the fort, leave by the west gateway. A broad, green track descends the fellside on a fairly steep gradient until it meets the metalled road as it follows a more twisting course to the valley floor. The original route followed a typical Roman custom by taking a zigzag course seventy yards north of the road, down a spur near Brotherilkeld Wood. West of Brotherilkeld the official route, according to Margary, has not been identified, and no road structure of Roman type has been found until the approach to the fort site three-quarters of a mile south of Ravenglass near Muncaster. It is assumed that the Roman road has been destroyed and ploughed out by cultivation of the valley flats.

In preparation of this section of the route, I decided, after consideration, to approach the problem from the fort site on the coast and the clear evidence of a Roman road at Holme Farm. From this point a long, straight lane heads north-east (although we must not assume too much from the fact that it is straight), up the ridge of Muncaster Fell, to continue by public footpath along the southern flank of the fell on raised ground above and overlooking the valley of the Esk, a far more logical and tactically desirable route than along the far wetter and possibly boggy valley bottom. From the end of this stretch just south of Eskdale Green, we are again on lower cultivated ground, but I have been able to plot a course along a series of paths and lanes by stream, waterfalls and woods, following for most part of the way an old packhorse route which eventually meets the present road near the cattle-grid at the foot of Hardknott Pass and our present position.

Just before the modern road reaches the valley floor there is a small car-park overlooking the gorge at Hardknott Gill. A small stone bridge, inscribed 'Jubilee Bridge 1977' crosses the gill at this point and, together with a signpost, indicates the route of a bridlepath to Dalesgarth and Muncaster. This is an old packhorse route adopted perhaps from an even older route and the one I have chosen to follow. Cross the gill by the bridge and turn up a rough boulder-strewn dry stream-bed. This, I admit, could be difficult if the stream is in full flood, as the original path higher on the right appears to have been swept away for a short distance. Pass over the two stiles to gain the fellside below the high crags of Birker Fell. A broad path lies straight ahead, soon to rise and climb up around the southern slopes of Harter Fell. Our way is a narrow track which drops slightly to head south-west along the edge of a narrow wood with a boundary wall on your right. Shortly, the path leaves the wall to head diagonally up the fellside to a gate in a dry-stone wall; a solitary holly tree lies beyond.

The narrow path now crosses the steep bracken-covered fellside on a constant level before fording a small stream to enter a plantation of young larch trees over a stile. A further stile marks the exit from the plantation, and the still narrow, but clear, path then passes along the edge of a mature wood which covers the still steep slopes to the left, whilst to the right open pastures, behind the dry-stone wall, lead down to the River Esk in the valley bottom below.

Note an unusual feature of the dry-stone walls of the Esk valley: most of the stones are of a rounded nature quite unlike so many of the Lakeland walls made up of angular and square-cornered blocks of brittle stone. The Esk valley walls are made mainly of granite, weathered into rounded cobbles, which reflect the fact that Eskdale represents the largest area of this rock in the Lake District.

The path leaves the wall slightly as it twists amongst the tall trees to a further wall crossing its path, where a high stile effects a crossing out of this wood. Immediately beyond the wall the route is cut by the fast-flowing, tumbling waters of Spothow Gill, but no difficulty should be experienced in crossing as numerous large stones and small boulders can be used as stepping-stones across the narrow gill. The path here is not clear for a short distance over boggy ground, but after a detour around the wet ground, head for the dry-stone wall on the same alignment as before, where a signpost indicates the way, with an alternative route to Whahouse Bridge. Our way continues along the previous alignment, in a westerly direction. The path dips and rises to cross a small stream by a ford as it continues through an open wood with a dry-stone wall still on the right, until a further well-maintained stile is reached. The route now crosses an open area along a fine, broad grass track, the plantations on the south side retreating up the higher slopes, the riverside pastures still with us, below the Eskdale Fells to the north.

Map 39

Use another, equally well-maintained stile here, and after crossing a small stream the route makes its way through a pasture, marked on the survey map as a sheepfold, but on the day of my last visit occupied by a herd of Cumbrian cattle. Cows, calves and, of course, the bull. 'Where is the bull?' is always my first thought in these circumstances, and there he was, two yards away, contentedly chewing without an evil thought in his mind. A few of the mothers eyed me rather suspiciously but that was all. A gate leads out of the pasture into an area of rough fell and bracken but the grass track is well defined after crossing two converging streams by shallow

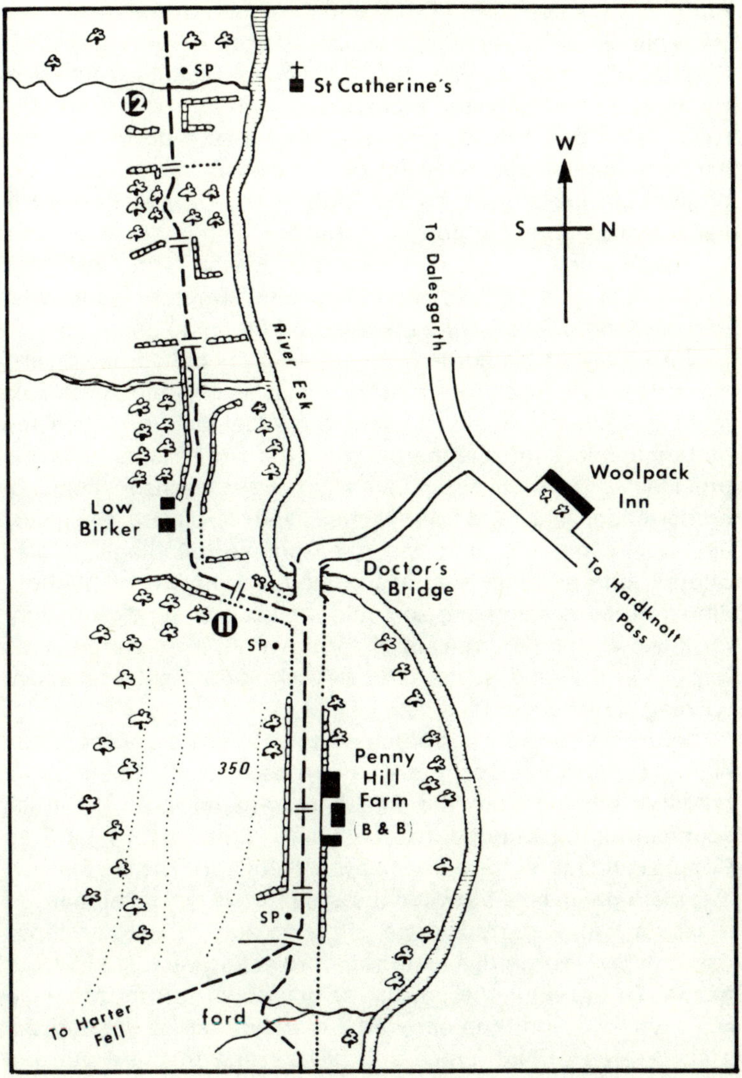
SP
St Catherine's
12
W
S
N
To Dalesgarth
River Esk
Woolpack
Inn
Low
Birker
Doctor's
Bridge
192
To
Hardknott
Pass
11
SP
Penny
Hill
Farm
(B & B)
350
SP
To Harter
Fell
ford

Map 39

fords. A track comes in from the high ground to the south, and the signpost by the next gate indicates a route from Harter Fell. A series of gates between dry-stone walls directs the route past Penny Hill Farm (bed and breakfast available) to a fenced farm road, its verges a medley of wild flowers of a dozen or more varieties. Across the valley lies the Woolpack Inn, although the original inn used to be on this side of the river at Penny Hill Farm, which certainly confirms the age of this ancient route.

Heading now almost due west, this fenced farm road leads to the Doctor's Bridge, so called after Doctor Tyson who widened the original old packhorse bridge in 1734 to provide easier access to his home at Penny Hill. Should you so desire, the bridge offers a dry crossing, back across the River Esk, making a short diversion to visit the Woolpack Inn, once the gathering place of shepherds and wool merchants. The inn provides a restricted but pleasant no-nonsense menu of home-made soup and sandwiches, and of course the usual liquid refreshments, in clean, pleasant surroundings. It also offers bed-and-breakfast accommodation with or without dinner in the evening and so could provide a breaking-off point for those wishing to break up the journey. A few hundred yards further up the road is the purpose-built youth hostel for those wishing more basic facilities.

Returning to the good doctor's bridge, cross and continue along the farm track on the southern bank of the Esk, a name probably derived from the British river-name Isca. The track soon leaves the wooded river course to climb gently past Crag Coppice and round the side of Low Birker Farm. The way is now a smooth green lane between dry-stone walls typical of many of these packhorse routes. Immediately on our left, craggy slopes rise steeply, with individual crags projecting almost over our heads. To the right the ground slopes down to the tree-lined river, whilst beyond the panorama marches across the horizon, a succession of high crags and pikes rising to the north and east, with Scafell dominating the immediate scene.

A footbridge and ford cross a small stream coming from the crags above known as Birker Force. The waterfall can be seen best from across the valley. The still well-defined track now crosses open ground for a short distance before passing through a gate into a small wood. Here the way becomes stony among the young trees; the river still keeps us company down the steep bank on our right. A further gate marks the end of the wood and once more we cross open ground, a smooth grass track between dense bracken. A dry-stone wall now joins us on our right for a short time, but on reaching another small stream the wall executes a right-angled turn down the fellside to the river. This is the path to the stepping-stones across to St Catherine's Chapel, dating back to the fourteenth century. Our way is straight ahead, but should you be tempted to visit the chapel, beware: the stepping-stones are more often than not under water and consequently slippy. The chapel can be reached an easier way, as I will explain later.

Map 40

After crossing the small stream, the track continues through a clearing surrounded by trees, and a further gate leads into a area of fir trees down through which flows a substantial stream crossed by a high foot-bridge. Higher upstream is the well-known and impressive waterfall of Stanley Force, sometimes referred to as Dalesgarth Force. The waterfall is one of the finest in the Lake District, with a fall of sixty feet. It lies within a small area of designated National Park Access Land and is open to visitors.

After passing through a gate to leave the wood, the track now crosses through a pasture to another gate leading into a farm lane, where a signpost indicates our way across a stile on the opposite side; the way to the right is the lane to Dalesgarth.

Dalesgarth Station is the terminus of the Ravenglass and Eskdale Railway, a privately owned miniature fifteen-inch-gauge track which is the only public transport service into the valley. Originally built over a hundred years ago by a Mr Ratcliffe to carry iron ore, it is now affectionately referred to as 'The Ratty' and for many years has carried thousands of walkers, campers and the like, as well as serving the local

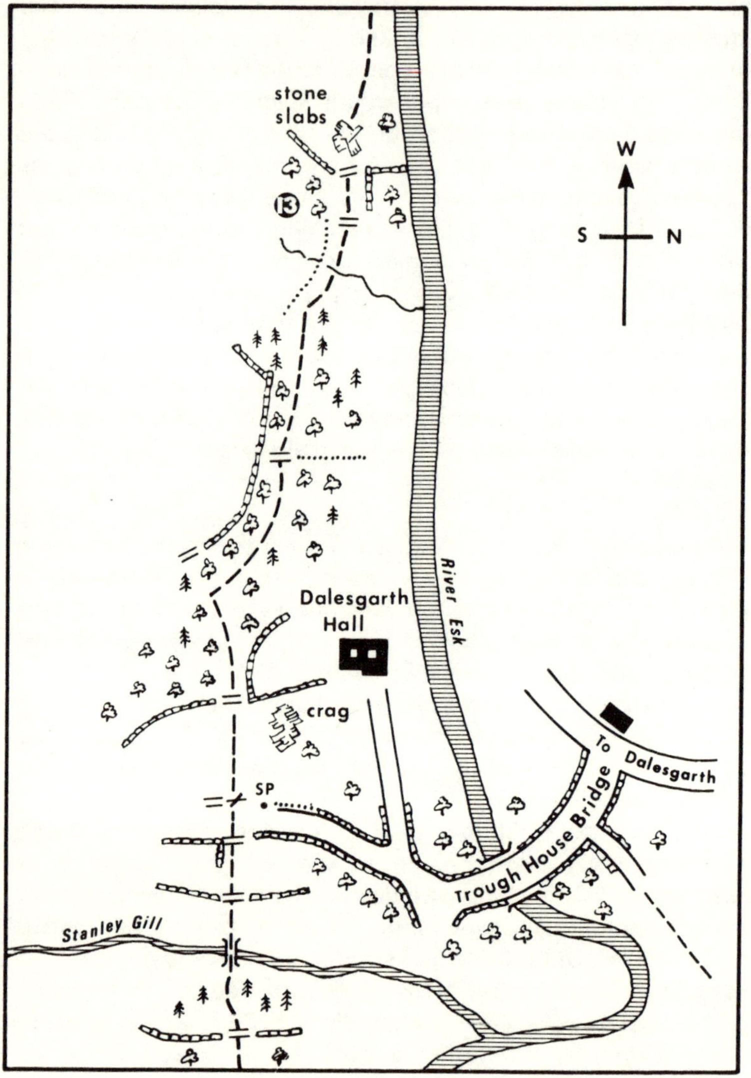
stone
slabs
W
S
N
13
River Esk
Dalesgarth
Hall
crag
To Dalesgarth
SP
Trough House Bridge
Stanley Gill

Map 40

communities of Irton and Eskdale Green. Now, unfortunately, its future is in doubt: a recent atomic radiation scare has kept many visitors away from the Cumbrian coast and has caused a severe drop in the revenue of the system, which relies heavily on visitors making the return trip along this beautiful stretch of track into the heart of this little-visited and unspoilt valley.

Should you wish to visit Dalesgarth, turn right along the lane and follow it past the entrance drive to Dalesgarth Hall, a semi-fortified building with parts dated back to the fourteenth century (notice the unusual rounded chimneys). Going over Trough House Bridge, which spans a deep gorge and is a popular swimming place, we pass a narrow bridlepath, the alternative route to St Catherine's Chapel. On reaching the main road, turn right to reach Dalesgarth Station, a few hundred yards beyond. The station café provides hot and cold snacks at very modest prices. Half a mile to the north-east of the station is the small village of Boot. Here can be found the village post office, a tea shop and the Burnmoor Inn. A restaurant is also situated at the crossroads of the Hardknott and Boot roads for those wishing a more substantial meal.

To return to the route, the way is indicated by a bridlepath sign to Forge Bridge. Cross over by the stile and follow the clear, broad green tack, past a high crag on the right and through the gate ahead into a shady wood. For those who have not seen Dalesgarth Hall along the route to the village, its top half can be seen to your right as you pass through, into the wood. The route drops down slightly along a stony path as it meanders and undulates between the tall, mature conifers of many types: larch, spruce and fir, as well as native oak and beech. The woodland path, now soft and springy under foot, maintains a generally westerly direction, with occasional glimpses of the fells to the south across the valley floor. The way passes through several gates, but the path is easy to follow and no difficulties should be encountered. Just over half a mile from the Hall, the route passes through a gate out of the wooded area, over a pathway of rock slabs to drop down onto a riverside path, the River Esk having turned in on a wide bend from the north. The path and the sparkling clear waters of the Esk continue side by side for several hundred yards before it turns northwards again. Our way continues along the same alignment through a grove of sycamore trees, past a small ruined farm dwelling and over a stile into an open pasture which affords views of the fells both north and south.

Map 41

On crossing the stile into the pasture, you can not but notice its excellent design and new condition; this is repeated many times over the next few miles, and whoever is responsible deserves to be congratulated.

The route now is between two fences for a short distance as the river rejoins us once more on the right. Immediately before crossing a second stile, note a small foot suspension bridge crossing the river, partially hidden by trees. This is a footpath leading to Eskdale Green and the Outward Bound Mountain School at Gate House. On crossing the stile our route enters another area of pastureland, passing Milkinstead Farm on the left with its small herd of brown-and-white cows. As we follow the farm track, the blast of a train whistle can often be heard as the small steam-train nears Eskdale Green Station just across the valley.

The farm track leaves the pasture to enter a further wooded area through the edge of Milkinstead Wood, the river still close by on the right. One more gate and stile, still of the same high quality, and a few yards bring us to the temporary end of this bridlepath as it meets the main road at Forge Bridge. A short distance across the bridge is the King George IV hotel, well worth a visit if the time is right; it was called 'The King of Prussia' until the events of 1914.

As you will see from the Ordnance Survey map, I was faced at Forge Bridge with something of a dilemma. Should I try to maintain the south-west alignment and risk the private road route over the river to the next public right of way at Muncaster Head or make a considerable diversion through Eskdale Green? I took the private road route, which as it turned out was no risk

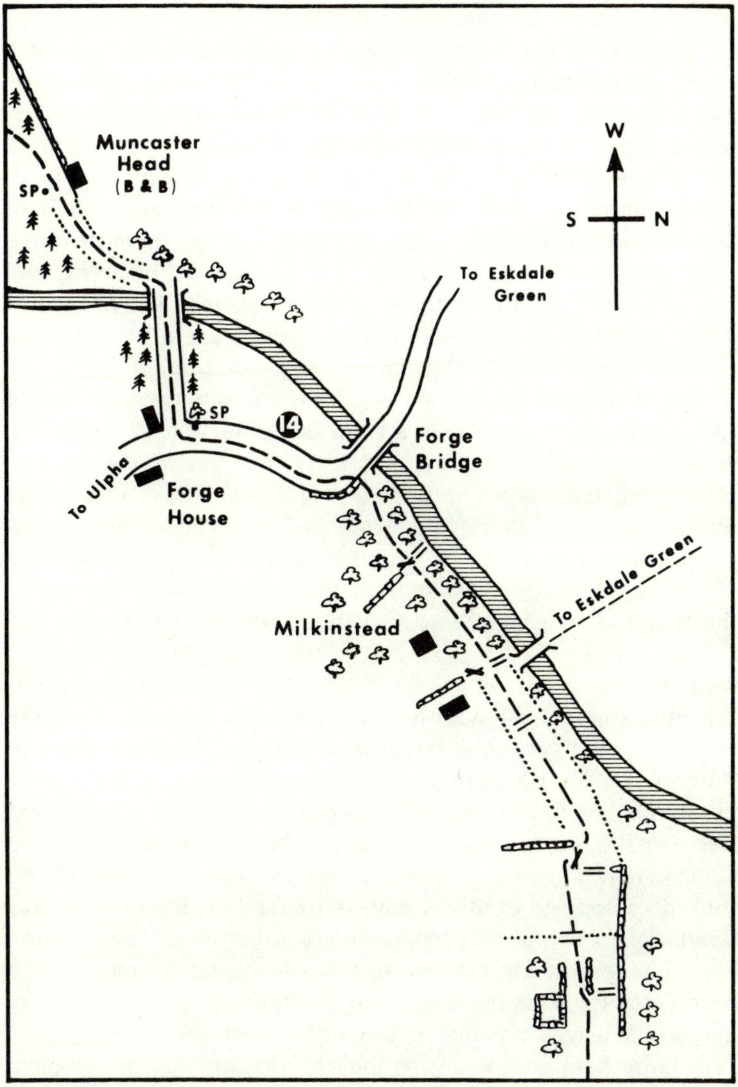
Muncaster
Head
(B & B)
SP
W
S
N
To Eskdale
Green
SP
14
Forge
Bridge
To Ulpha
Forge
House
To Eskdale Green
Milkinstead

Map 41

at all and is by far the better route.

Turn left at the main road and in less than a quarter of a mile, before reaching Forge House, which is on the left of the road, a drive, marked 'Private Road to Muncaster Head', appears on the right; turn down this and cross the river by a fine stone bridge. Continue along the drive with banks of rhododendron bushes on the right and a new plantation of conifers on the left. The drive continues through open pastures until the farmhouse of Muncaster Head is reached. Here bed and breakfast, with or without an evening meal, is available at very modest cost, but should you contemplate a break at this point, I would strongly advise you to book beforehand.

The farm buildings have a very interesting history, for during the last century there was an iron-smelting works and forge here, using local iron ore and charcoal, hence the several references to the word here about, e.g. Forge House and the fell above the farm bearing the name of Forge Hills. Just beyond the house is a new footpath guide-post indicating the way I had come as the route to Dalesgarth, showing at least consent to the usage even if it is not an established right of way.

Map 42

The next stage of the walk is as delightful as the last and, in my opinion, could very well have been adopted from the original Roman route. The farm track makes for easy walking as it gently climbs to the contour which it is to follow for the next two miles, a few feet up from the river bottom with the wooded slopes of Muncaster Fell rising steeply above. After passing through a coppice of mixed mature trees, the vista to the south opens up to reveal rich pasturelands which lead down to the river, unseen behind the veil of trees lining its banks, and the rough slopes of the far ridge with its undulating series of rocky crags like waves advancing towards the shore.

A large flock of ewes with their lambs and nearby a typical herd of beef cows with attendant calves graze the summer pastures.

After passing these pastures farmed from Muncaster Head

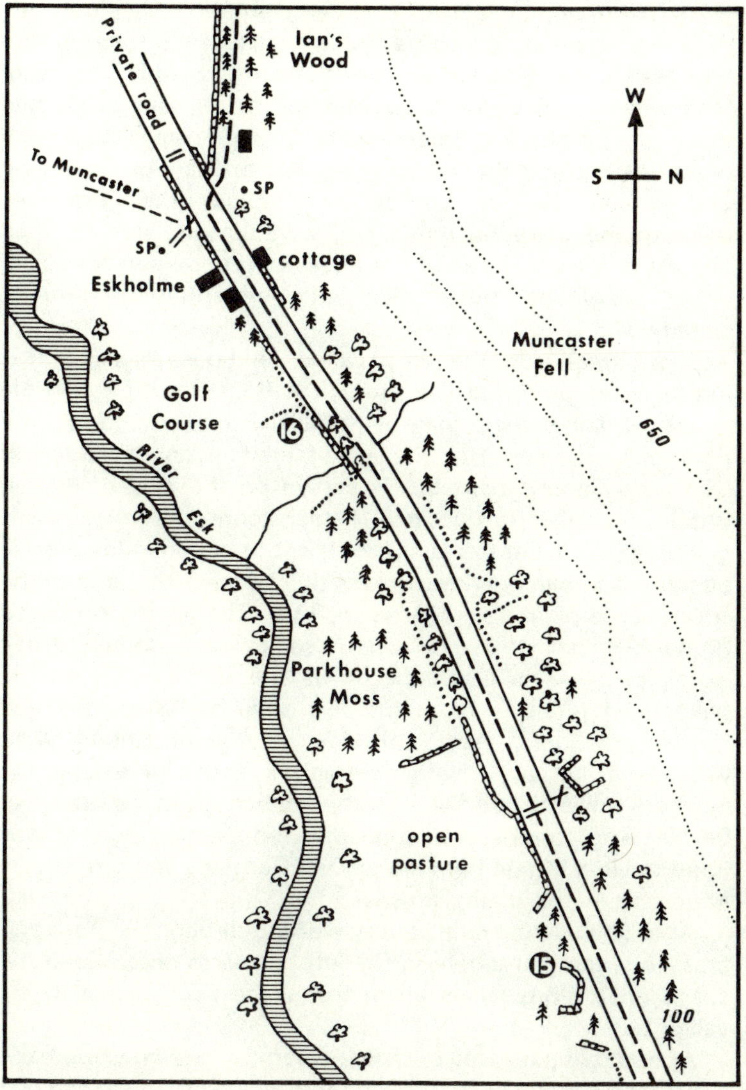
Private road
Ian's Wood
W
S
N
To Muncaster
SP
SP
cottage
Eskholme
Muncaster Fell
Golf Course
16
650
River Esk
Parkhouse Moss
open pasture
15
100

Map 42

Farm, the route now passes between plantations on either side of track, but unlike some forest walks this one is not oppressive: the wide selection of trees with their variety of foliage make every step full of interest and pleasure. Here and there groups of giant rhododendron bushes display their lush blossoms in every shade of pink against the dark green of pine and spruce. Twisted English oaks spread their branches beneath the towering noble firs, wild flowers are scattered liberally along the verge of the forest where the sun can reach them, foxgloves, buttercups, stitchwort, ladies' fingers, speedwell.

The plantation to the left is called Parkhouse Moss, so it is logical to assume that the site of the Roman pottery and tile works is somewhere nearby, officially referred to as the Parkhouse Pottery. The site is not marked on the standard Ordnance Survey maps but is shown on the map of Roman Britain, ten miles to one inch. A four-figure map reference is given, SD1398, but this is not sufficient to pin-point the precise position, so I can only assume for the moment that it is to the south of the plantation near to the river. The pottery produced Romano-British coarse wares used by the Roman army; examples of plates, jars, cups, bowls and tiles used for roofing have been found at both the fort sites at Ravenglass and Hardknott. Coarse-ware potteries in Roman Britain were usually set up by private contractors eager to exploit the northern military market, which, as has been pointed out before, was considerable. The finer red Samian pottery was imported into Britain from France and Germany and can be very important in the dating process.

After about half a mile of easy walking through the trees and blossoms, the plantation on the left comes to an end and the scene once more opens up to reveal the river course in the valley below.

After passing an area of timber clearance, we now approach a dwelling called Eskholme, no doubt connected with the golf course below; Yew Tree Cottage is opposite. The way is metalled, and after a few hundred yards a gate and sign indicate that the road is now private. Our route is along the bridlepath marked 'To Chapel Hill' on the right; a further route on the left leads to Muncaster Castle. The bridlepath, now a narrow track, heads diagonally up the fellside – it is obviously a long time since anyone on horseback took this route.

Map 43

The track climbs quite steeply between closely planted young conifers, their branches often meeting overhead, so low that it is often necessary to crouch below them to make progress. The route to the top western shoulder of the ridge is just over half a mile, but it seems a long half mile as we struggle uphill between trees and high bracken, with just occasional glimpses of the valley below, through the trees. A dry-stone wall keeps us company a little way to the left. The path in parts is rather boggy as tiny streams cross it on their way down the hillside, but it is clear and easy to follow, and the spirits lighten at the sight of a small spruce tree festooned with a flowering honeysuckle. Three-quarters of the way up we pass a group of buildings behind the wall, surrounded by tall, majestic conifers. At last the summit of our short climb is reached, marked by an iron gate through which we pass to begin the descent down into the valley.

You might ask the question: if this is indeed basically the original Roman route, why did the Roman engineers climb the hill from the fort and then continue the road down the other side, rather than take the more direct route along the lower ground? The answer is that we don't know why, but we do know that the Roman road planners did like to site their roads on the higher ground rather than the lower, and a high sighting point was important to decide upon the overall alignment. You will also note from the survey map that there is an area just north-east of Muncaster Castle near a bend in the river named Eskholme Marsh: even the present road takes a wide sweep around it. So who knows whether this whole area was subject to flooding all those centuries ago, and if the Roman surveyors simply took the simple precaution of heading directly for the

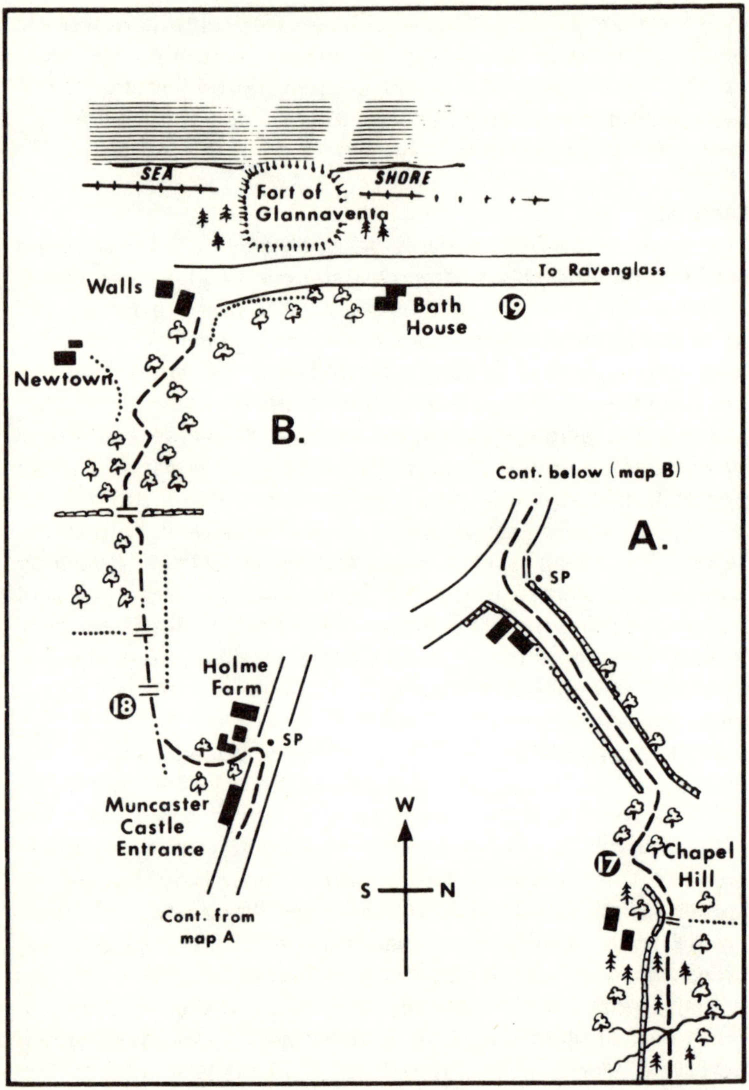
SEA
SHORE
Fort of Glannaventa
To Ravenglass
Walls
Bath House
19
Newtown
B.
Cont. below (map B)
A.
SP
Holme Farm
18
SP
Muncaster Castle Entrance
W
S
N
17
Chapel Hill
Cont. from map A

Map 43

high ground before turning the road onto its final north-easterly alignment?

On passing through the iron gate we get our first sight of the sea since the summit of Hardknott and the final stretch of the river estuary, no doubt a welcome change of scenery for our Roman travellers after their long journey from the fort at Brougham, or perhaps further north on the wall itself. The track makes its way across an open woodland before joining a broad lane which heads in a straight line down the hillside between dry-stone walls: this is Fell Lane. With open ground to the right and woodland on the left for most of the way, the lane steadily descends on an easy gradient until the main road is reached.

To continue the south-west alignment would mean cutting across the Muncaster Castle Estate to the established route south-east of Holme Farm, a course of action which may not be popular, so a short diversion is advised. Take the main road towards Ravenglass, passing on the right St Michael's County Guest House, a former school (a very reasonable tariff) and shortly afterwards the lodge to Muncaster Castle.

Muncaster Castle, the home of the Pennington family since the thirteenth century, is open to the public. Although the building itself is Victorian, built in 1862, it was built onto a medieval pele tower. The main features today are the attractive array of landscaped gardens, a fine collection of paintings, including one of an impression of Hardknott Castle in Roman times, and antique furniture.

Shortly after passing the lodge, by Holme Farm a signpost indicates a bridlepath to Ravenglass. Turn along it behind a group of barns and down a woodland path for a short distance. Turn right, pass through a gate onto a fenced track, and through a further gate into an open field. This stretch is directly in line with the previous alignment along Fell Lane and the section mentioned by Margary as a proved part of the original route, although there is nothing to identify on the surface. Continue straight ahead with a fence on your right, passing a small fenced swamp area on the left. Enter the extensive wood through the gate in the boundary wall. Follow the woodland path as it winds its way through the trees and shrubs before entering a short, straight drive. Turn right at the eventual junction, and right again at the next fork. The plantation, now immediately on your left, covers the Roman fort platform; some of the mature trees are now being felled, although the remaining root systems are not likely to make any future excavation an easy task.

The Roman fort of Glannaventa (Grid Ref. SD0895), 'the town on the bank', was first mentioned in print by the Tudor antiquary William Camden in 1600. An account of 1860 mentions the fort enclosure as still visible, and finds of coins and pottery. In 1860 the Furness Railway Line was cut through the fort platform, and further finds were made. 1885–6 saw excavations by Lord Muncaster which revealed that the fort buildings had been robbed. Later a dense tree-planting made further excavations difficult. Francis Haverfield, in 1915, identified the fort as Glannaventa, the official start (or finish) of the Tenth Antonine Itinerary (see note 4) via Hardknott, Ambleside and beyond.

The famous archaeologist W.G. Collingwood (1889–1943), always held the belief that Glannaventa was Agricolan, built in AD 79–80, and in fact was the base for his proposed invasion of Ireland. It is generally now accepted from recent evidence that Agricola bypassed the Lake District in his major drive northwards and that the fort at Ravenglass was not built until the reign of Hadrian, AD 117–38. Late Roman pottery and coins suggest that it was held late into the fourth century. The only known garrison was the First Cohort Morinorum and Cersiacorum, raised from two tribes who lived in the Boulogne area of France. It was sent to Britain with Cerialist in AD 71 and is recorded in the *Notitia* as being stationed at Glannaventa. A lead seal of the First Cohort Aelia Classica, a unit raised from sailors, was found at Ravenglass, but there is no evidence that they were ever stationed there.

A further half mile towards the village we come to the Roman bath house, marked on the map as Walls Castle. It lies outside the fort, a not unusual situation. Parts of the building, which has never been excavated, still stand to the height of $12\frac{1}{2}$ feet, making it the best-preserved Roman structure in the north of England. A wooden fence surrounds it, but no notice as to its origin or history is to be seen, which is a great pity. Such important archaeological remains surely deserve at least the minor expenditure of a well-presented plan and explanatory text.

It has been suggested that there was a large civilian settlement at Ravenglass which no doubt developed around the fort and natural harbour which was situated at the confluence of the rivers Esk and Mite. It would be inhabited by traders and families of the fort garrison, whose purpose would have been not only to protect the port and its role in the coastal shipping system of the time but also to keep order in the immediate area. As already stated, there is evidence that the fort was occupied until late in the fourth century, as were most of the forts along Hadrian's Wall, having been under persistent pressure for many years from the Picts, Scots and Attacotti. The main fury seems to have fallen on the northern frontier and the western coastlands. There is in fact evidence that the barrack blocks in the Ravenglass fort were destroyed by fire sometime between AD 200 and 210, after which they were very quickly rebuilt; although there is nothing to indicate the cause of the fire, enemy action cannot be ruled out.

The full story of the end to effective occupation of the forts of the north and the ultimate fate of the remaining garrisons is obscure, and any precise date unknown, but although the official connection of Britain with the Roman Empire ended in AD 410, the Roman framework and civilization of the province were in some degree maintained until 442 and possibly well beyond. In the late fifth century the leadership passed to Ambrosius Aurelianus and after him to the legendary Arthur – very little is known of either. The Dark Ages had arrived.

The small seaside town of Ravenglass is a request halt stop on the scenic coastal rail route between Barrow and Carlisle. It contains two pubs, the Pennington Arms, with a comprehensive range of catering plus accommodation, and 'The Ratty' named after the railway of that name, with a more modest menu. There is a small railway museum and information centre which has an up-to-date list of all types of accommodation and places of interest in the area.

A small village these days, Ravenglass was of much greater importance in the thirteenth century, when the first market charter was granted. It was a successful port doing a busy trade with Ireland and the entry port for the smuggling trade which made the long haul over the Lakeland passes with their trains of packhorses. Today the harbour channel has silted up, and most of the sea-going activity is confined to daily hire for fishing parties. The sand dunes to the north of the estuary are an important nature reserve, the breeding grounds of black-headed gulls and terns.

CHAPTER 6

Whitley Castle (Roman name unknown) near Alston to Kirkby Thore (Bravoniacum). Margary's route 84. 17 miles.

It was my intention when planning this book that all routes would radiate from a central point, the Roman fort of Brocavum at Brougham Castle. The plan proved practical until I commenced the preparation of this chapter. For the first few miles the route presents no problems as it passes along quiet country lanes, through small interesting villages and isolated hamlets until it reaches the base of the high plateau of Melmersby Fell. It was at this point that I was forced to revise my plans. The route (as shown on the Ordnance Survey maps) up the very steep and rough slopes of Ardale Side is impossible to detect, and the almost complete lack of identifiable features makes it extremely difficult to produce a guide which would fulfil the needs of the inexperienced fell-walker. On my last attempt to solve the problem I had my first experience of the fury of the notorious Helm Wind, an unusually strong wind peculiar to the district, which howled down the fellside from the north-east accompanied by sheeting rain, which incidentally trapped me in my small one-man tent for fourteen hours – a factor which may very well have been contributory to my final decision to abandon the south-to-north route.

In contrast, the route south from Whitley Castle has a long, gentle ascent of the high fells, along a route traceable on the ground for much of the way and consequently easy to follow; it also has the immediate advantage of a thousand-foot elevated starting point.

About the road

The road we are to follow is second only to the High Street route for its seclusion and the heights which it attains across the virtually untouched moors of the northern Pennines. Considerable remains are to be seen as it crosses the high plateau where wind and weather have stripped away the surface materials to leave exposed the original rock foundation stones exactly as laid by the Roman road-makers nineteen hundred years ago. To date the road is difficult, for although we know that the fort at Kirkby Thore was founded by Agricola in AD 79–80, this northern link road was probably not built until later in the Hadrianic period and the building of the forts at Brampton and Carvorum further north.

The fort at Whitley Castle is thought to have been built to house a garrison responsible for the security of the lead and silver mines, an important industry in the area. These mines were usually the charge of the military, although in the later period they were sometimes leased out to civilian contractors. The mines were, in the main, open-cast, and the workers criminals serving sentences for their crimes. The lead extracted was extensively used for waterproofing and plumbing, whilst the small quantity of silver, less than one per cent, was exclusively the property of the state. The road was most likely built to link the industry to the forts and settlements to the south. One of the duties of the troops of the garrison would no doubt be to escort the trains of pack mules carrying their loads of ingots over the high, desolate moors.

The route leaves the fort at Whitley Castle and heads south along a broad track in part adopted by the Pennine Way. After crossing Gilderdale Burn it steadily climbs the slopes of Park Fell to pass over a ridge and eventually drops down to reach the A686, a distance of approximately four miles.

The route crosses the road to begin its long, steady climb to the top of Melmersby Fell. This is a very desolate stretch, magnificent in its remoteness, with no shelter for at least seven miles: a fine high-level walk which must *not* be attempted if the visibility is poor. The first two miles area along a broad, firm track after which the route becomes less clear and relies on a series of small cairns marking the way until the summit is reached. From here good visibility is essential to negotiate the steep but mercifully short descent to Ardale Beck and the lower ground of the Eden Valley. The last part of the route to Kirkby Thore has been adopted for much of the way by the quiet country lanes previously mentioned.

Spring and summer would probably be the best times to undertake the walk, but emphasis must be placed on clear conditions prevailing at the time. Avoid the shooting season as the route passes through extensive grouse moors on either side of the A686. Clothing worn should be as mentioned in Chapter 4, and stout boots are essential.

Alston, the highest market town in England, lies on a hillside two miles south-east of Whitley Castle and would make an excellent base from which to start the walk. Once the centre of the lead-mining industry, it now concentrates on providing a wide range of facilities for the passing traveller, whether he be a hardy walker of the Pennine Way or motorist touring the area. There are at least eight public houses in the attractive town with its cobbled main street, several hotels within the immediate district and numerous bed-and-breakfast establishments. All the pubs provide meals as well as liquid refreshments, and there are also a number of cafés and shops. Five roads meet in the town, and it is readily accessible from both the M6 and the A1(M). Most of the facilities are available all the year round, with skiing becoming increasingly popular as the surrounding high fells receive more than their fair share of winter snows.

The Route

Map 44

The site of the Roman fort at Whitley Castle (its Roman name is not known, although the Victorian antiquarian W.T. Watkins suggests that it may have been Glannibanta) is situated approximately two miles north-west of the busy market town of Alston, two hundred yards off the A689, Alston to Brampton

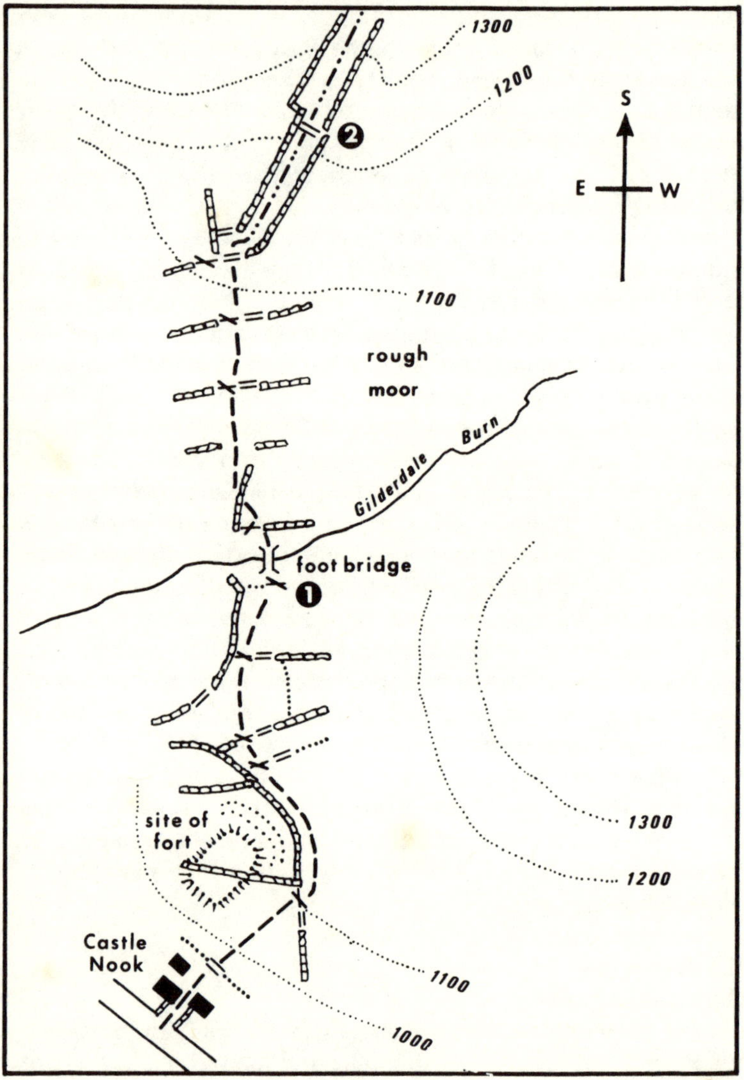
1300
1200
S
E
W
2
1100
rough
moor
Gilderdale Burn
foot bridge
1
site of
fort
1300
1200
Castle
Nook
1100
1000

Map 44

road, and half a mile into the county of Northumberland (Map reference NY 6949). The site covers an area of three acres, and the excavations of 1957–8 revealed evidence that the fort was occupied between the middle of the second and the third century. Inscriptions tell us that in the third century the fort was garrisoned by the Second Cohort of Nerviorum, originally recruited in Belgium. The site is particularly noted for its well-preserved series of seven defensive ditches situated on the western side of the fort, similar to those found at the fort at Ardock in Tayside.

The site can be reached by passing through the yard of Castle Nook Farm on the left of the main road, where a gate gives access to a field; the fort site is situated on the raised ground to the left. A dry-stone wall bisects the fort platform; pass through a gap in this wall to view the defensive ditches on the west side. The Roman road passes the fort on the eastern side; our way is by the gate or stile through the wall surrounding the site around the western side. The clear track passes through two more gates before dropping down towards Gilderdale Burn. Here the track is badly eroded. Follow the wire fence down the slope to a gate and stile in a stone wall, after which the now rough track drops steeply down to the footbridge across the beck.

As we approach the beck, the way ahead, a broad green path, can be seen climbing up the opposite slope. The well-maintained footbridge with a stile at either end crosses the beck and at the same time the old county boundary between Northumberland and Cumberland. Follow the track up the steep slope, through a ruined stone wall and onto the broad green path. The fine pathway of short grass cuts a straight line up the rough fellside passing over two high stiles with unusual curved handholds. This section of the route is that described as part of the Pennine Way and is so indicated by the line on the 1:25,000 Series map, of which there is no evidence on the ground.

The third high stile is for those following the path down to the Alston road; our way is through the gate ajoining the stile and into the broad, walled lane. Here we turn right and begin a long gradual ascent of the western slopes of Park Fell. The lane so typical of an old drovers' road could well have been adopted from the Roman route as it runs straight and true almost due south-west towards a gap between two peaks.

Map 45

The walled lane is approximately one mile long of good, easy walking, although it has become rutted in places. At the end of the lane a gate gives access to a rough, open moor. Here the track disappears entirely, but by keeping the dry-stone wall on the right, the same alignment is maintained until it angles away down the fellside. Continue towards the gap between the two hills, taking a route over the rough ground which rises slightly towards another stone wall moving in from the left. This wall leads to where a wire fence bars our route. A line of shooting butts along the edge of the ridge to the right reminds us that this could be a restricted area at certain times of the year. A small well-fastened gate presents something of a problem but the low wire fence none at all.

The next section of just under a mile in length can be rather hard going as there is no trackway, and the route crosses a peat moor thickly covered with heather. Keep fairly close to the stone wall on the left; the occasional sheep track helps to negotiate the crossing. As the ground rises slightly, a dry-stone wall appears across the route. A partially hidden stile is to be found a few yards to the right as you approach the wall. Beyond the wall the way becomes easier, and a track appears, only to lead off to a gap in the left-hand wall. Keep straight on, with the wall now close on your left, across the flat moor. The sound of passing traffic warns us that the A686 is nearby, below the ridge.

A fence comes up from the left: from here the true route continues its course diagonally down the fellside to cross the road just east of a wooded gully. It is possible to continue this alignment down the fellside, crossing on its way through a ruined dry-stone wall to a further wall (which has to be climbed

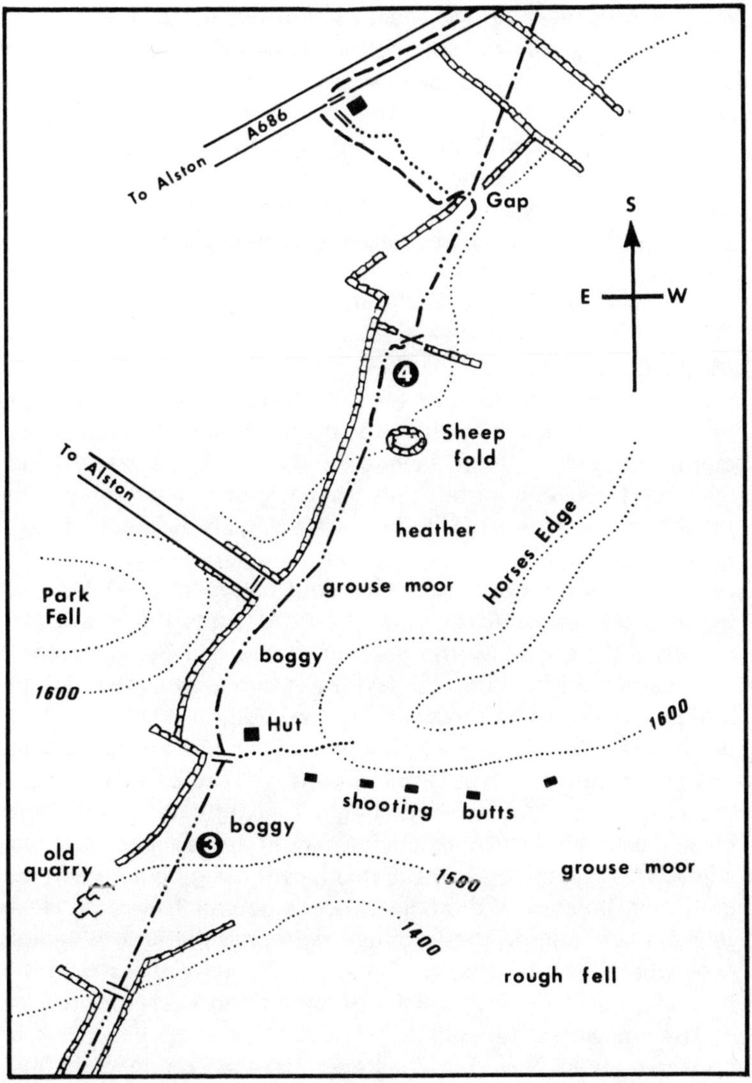

To Alston
A686
Gap
S
E
W
4
Sheep fold
To Alston
heather
Horses Edge
grouse moor
Park Fell
boggy
1600
Hut
1600
shooting butts
boggy
3
old quarry
1500
grouse moor
1400
rough fell

Map 45

over) before reaching the main road. An easier way is to pass through the gap in the wall and head downhill to the left of the wire fence. Two gates give access to the A686 by a farm building. Alston is three miles away by road.

The next section of the route is by far the most interesting but at the same time the most desolate as it crosses the barren moors of Hard Rigg Edge and Melmersby Fell and across the sweeping slopes of Ousbydale and Ardale Side. There is no shelter and the chance of meeting another individual in the whole seven miles extremely unlikely.

Map 46

Having reached the road by the farm building, continue along it for just one mile to where a thickly wooded gully drops down the fellside. If you have continued to follow the original alignment, obviously the gully, which can not be missed, is much nearer. A few yards beyond the gully is a rough lane leading diagonally down the fell. Immediately across the narrow valley the route up the far slope can be clearly seen as a broad green track. After a few hundred yards the lane turns slightly right to follow the contour of the hill. By the second wall leading off the lane is a gate. Pass through this to continue straight down the fell towards the beck below: this is marked on the map as a footpath although there is no path to be seen on the ground. There is an alternative route to the beck crossing which follows the original alignment much more closely and is much more obvious when approached from the south. This can be found by climbing over the gate between the gully and the start of the lane; proceed downhill, keeping close to boundary wall on the left; bear right past the first telegraph pole where a farm track can be seen; this leads directly to the ford and, although not official, is by far the easier route.

The crossing of Rowgill Burn was by footbridge according to my survey map, and Margary states that the Romans also built a bridge here, but there is no sign of either to be seen today. After negotiating a crossing (not too difficult a task), the stone-based track executes a typical zigzag up the bank before

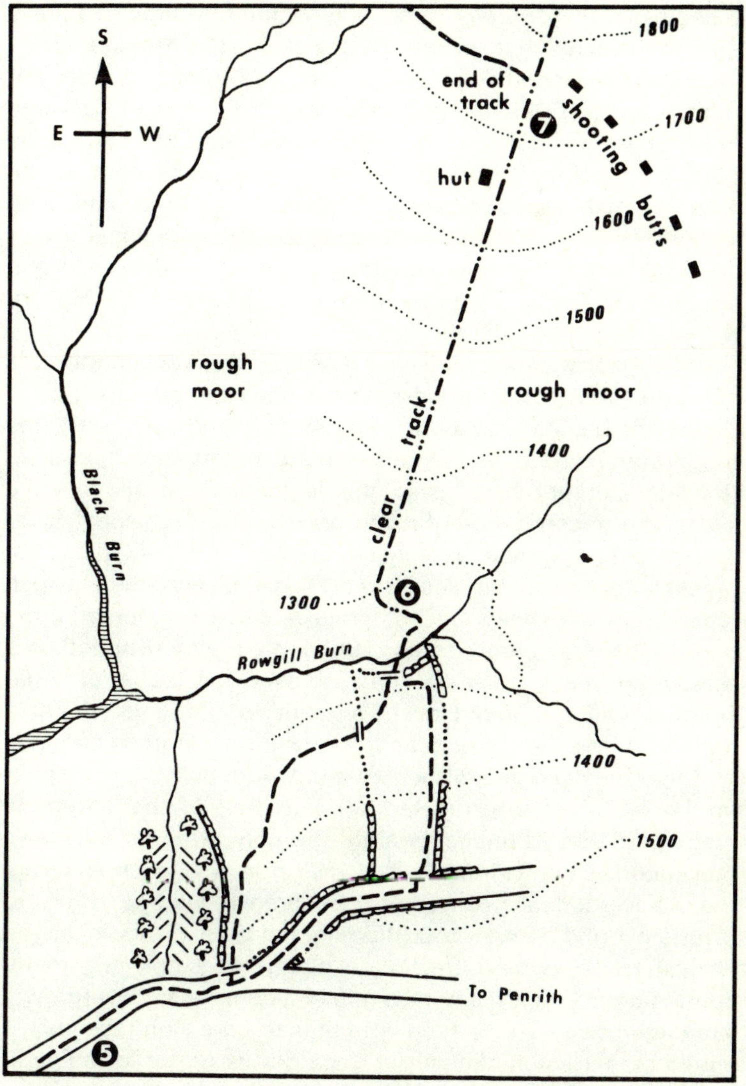
S
E
W
1800
end of
track
shooting
butts
1700
hut
1600
1500
rough
moor
rough moor
clear
track
1400
Black
Burn
1300
Rowgill Burn
1400
1500
To Penrith

Map 46

it begins its long, steady climb, and for the first time one really gets the feeling that we are now walking the Maiden Way : 'Mai-Dun', the great ridge way which used to stretch from the Roman fort of Galacum at Overborrow to the fort at Carvoran north of Whitley Castle, but which now bears the name only between the Castle and Kirkby Thore. The stone base of the road is much exposed where the surface material has been washed away and nature held at bay by the occasional use of the track by tractors of the modern shepherd on his rounds and shooting parties who use the route to reach their butts high on the slopes of the fell.

To the north lie the slopes of Hartside, cars reduced to dots climbing slowly over the pass; to the east, the bare heights of Cross Fell and its neighbours, and to the south and west, the rough barren moors bearing a sprinkling of flowering heather in the late summer heat. Even the few scattered sheep were silent, the uncanny quiet broken only by the occasional flurry and chuckle of grouse as they reluctantly left the shade of the bracken from almost under my feet. A scene very little changed (apart from the sheep and the grouse), since the Roman army passed this way centuries ago. Suddenly reality returned as a screaming mass of metal hurtled over the ridge at what seemed like head-height level, Tornadoes of the Royal Air Force and our roman route appear to be sharing common ground.

The track becomes rutted and more worn as it climbs higher up the fell, a small corrugated hut and a line of shooting butts waiting for the 'Glorious Twelfth' the only reminder of man's presence. At approximately one mile from the beck crossing, the track suddenly turns left, one branch leading down to Smittergill and another to a shooting hut behind the ridge. The Roman route carries straight on along the same alignment, continuing to climb but now almost completely overgrown. Although traces can be seen from time to time along the way, it would be extremely difficult to trace if it were not for a line of small stone cairns marking the route.

Map 47

The road heads directly up the fellside. The cairns, widely spaced, indicate the way. The route should not be attempted if the visibility is poor, for, as already stated, the cairns are only small and are not easily spotted in reduced conditions. It has been suggested that the use of compass bearings would be of value in this type of situation, but to me a compass is a gadget, and a man on the hills should rely on his own sense of direction and what he can see, not on a gadget – apart from the fact that most people are not familiar with the finer points of magnetic variations and deviations which are in themselves suspect in an area of considerable mineral deposits. Solitary fell-walking has often been roundly condemned. 'Always walk with others,' they say. This is excellent advice for the inexperienced or those who lack ordinary commonsense and, as we say in Lancashire, plain gumption. The man or woman (and here I quote the king of all fell-wanderers, A. Wainwright) who walks alone enjoys the greatest rewards: he sees and feels and senses the mood of the hills, and it is no coincidence that they are usually people of abundant commonsense, initiative and imagination. To a man in a conducted party, the mountains are prose; to the man travelling alone, they are poetry.

As we approach the edge of the high ridge, it is easy to see why the Roman surveyors chose this route: the slopes to the east are littered with peat hags, a gathering-ground for the waters of the Black Burn, a tributary of the South Tyne River. The Roman route becomes clear as we near the summit of the ridge: an extremely well-preserved stretch of road cuts across the fell below the ridge of loose stone – certainly no shortage of building material here.

The agger here is two to three feet high and twenty-one feet wide, with larger stones along the edge. Where the road is covered, the route is shown particularly clearly by the scorched grass. No doubt the stony ground of the ridge has helped to preserve this section of the road, and a high tribute should be paid to those who built it so many years ago. Who they were we have no way of knowing for sure, but it would not be too

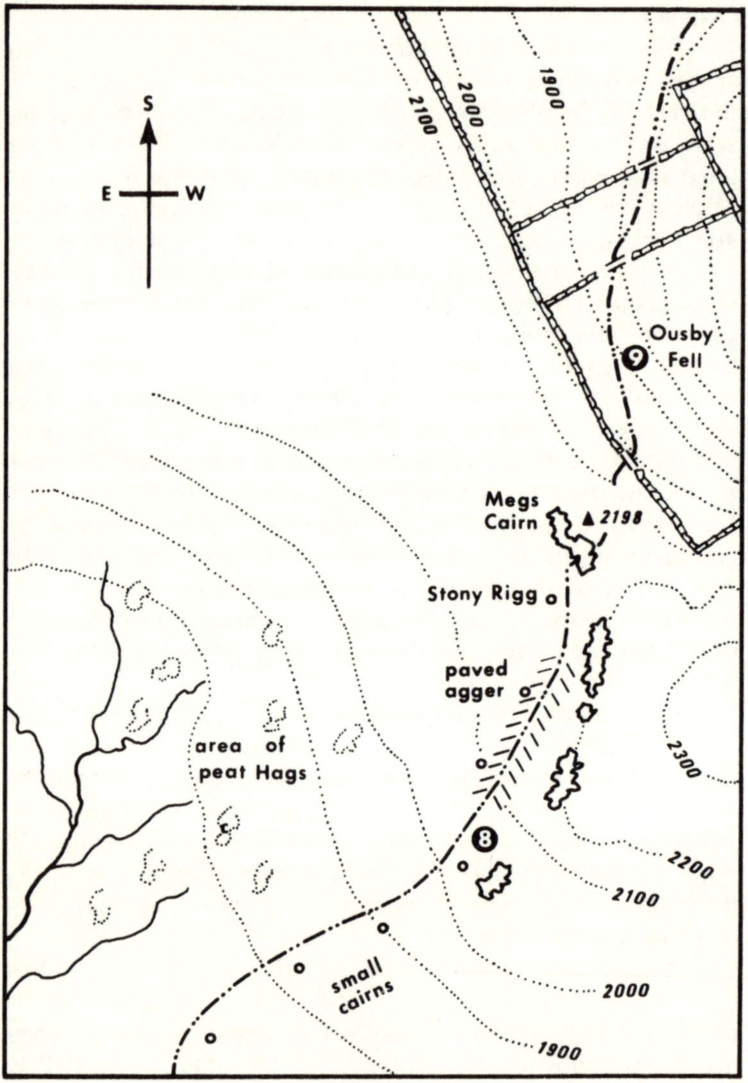
S
E
W
2100
2000
1900
Ousby
Fell
9
Megs
Cairn
2198
Stony Rigg
paved
agger
area of
peat Hags
2300
8
2200
2100
2000
small
cairns
1900

Map 47

unlikely that units from the auxiliary garrisons of the forts along the Stainmore Gap were involved, working under the supervision of an expert from one of the legions. We do know from scrawled inscriptions that two centurions of the Second and Twentieth Legions where present nearby, supervising the cutting of stone for the rebuilding of the fort at Kirkby Thore around the same time as the building of this road. These auxiliary troops came from all parts of the Roman Empire, and there is evidence to show that they would have included men from Spain, Gaul, Germany, Greece and as far away as Syria, the latter being a unit of archers stationed at Kirkby Thore.

As the route reaches the top of the ridge, sit awhile under the foot of Meg's Cairn to view the completely new vista which has revealed itself. Immediately before us is the broad bowl-shaped sweep of Ousbydale with the faint track of our route crossing its higher slopes; a spur of three small hills descends into the wide, fertile valley of the River Eden, a patch-work quilt of green meadows, ripening grain and broad-leafed trees. To the far west can be seen ridge upon ridge of the Lakeland hills, whilst to the north on a clear day there is a glimpse of Solway Firth.

From Meg's Cairn (who was Meg?) the route descends the rough fell to a gate in the dry-stone wall just below the ridge; it then continues diagonally across the slope to a further gate, and beyond that to a third gate. The track along this section is very faint and more easily identified from the distance than underfoot, the constructed road being overgrown and invisible in the soft, peaty ground. Our next reference point along the route is the outer corner of a fell boundary wall. These boundary walls can be invaluable in the process of route-plotting and, providing one is equipped with the 1:25,000 scale map which show the boundaries, it is almost impossible to get lost. The secret is to know exactly one's position on the map at all times. From the corner of the wall, continue along the same alignment. There is no track. Take care not to drift down but to maintain the same level along the contour of the fell and pass through a shallow gap between two small hills. An old disused quarry lies just off the route to the left.

Map 48

The view to the west, which was obscured after dropping down from the cairn, is again revealed as the route traverses a natural terrace overlooking the valley below. It was here that I was able to observe the Helm Bar at close hand. The Helm Bar is a long cloud which hangs motionless down the Eden Valley when the winds blow strong from the north-east. It stops, so it is said, the Helm Wind crossing the river. Just how true this is I cannot say, but there it was on this particular day, hanging motionless at the same height as my position on the terrace, whilst the north-east wind was doing its best to blow me into space.

The next reference point is a small ruined stone building situated at the meeting of two boundaries. This can be found by continuing along the terrace until a wire fence is encountered and then following it downhill. Pass through the gate in the fence where a partially hidden light railway track can be detected heading down the slope – the track no doubt once used to carry materials to and from the quarry further up the fell. A scar on the fell above marks the place where a prehistoric stone axe was found in 1880, referred to on the map as 'Man at Edge' and evidence of early man's presence in these inhospitable hills.

The Roman route, according to the survey map, cuts diagonally across the fell to drop directly down the steep side of Ardale, crossing the beck where it reaches level ground, but apart from a fragment of what could be the remains of an agger a few yards from the gate, there is no indication of the precise route. This was one of the problems when approaching the fell from the south, as a slight deviation going uphill could lead to difficulties in re-establishing contact with the route. Our way is to follow the tramway down the fell to where it passes through a fence. A gate leads to a track which continues down the fell to the right of a conical hill: turn off, to the left of the hill, and down a cleft below the scree slope. Although there is no track

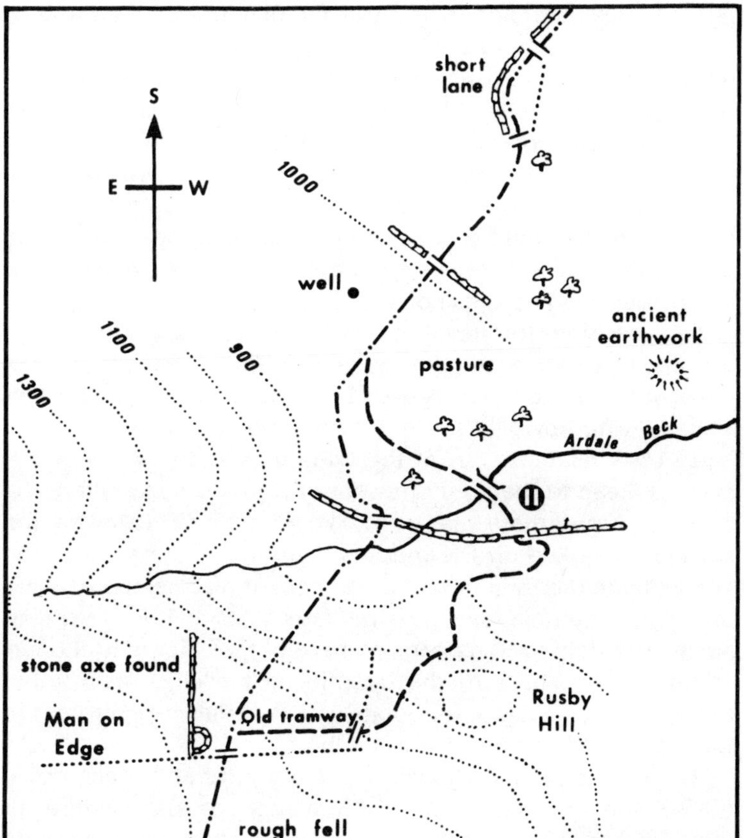
short
lane
S
E
W
1000
well
ancient
earthwork
1100
900
pasture
1300
Ardale Beck
11
stone axe found
Rusby
Hill
Man on
Edge
Old tramway
rough fell
Old
Quarry
1700
Muska
Hill
10

Map 48

as such, this natural route is easily negotiated as it descends to the foot of the fell. I have tried several different routes up the fellside from Ardale Beck, including the official one, which to my mind is the most difficult, and I cannot imagine the Roman engineers building a road directly up a one foot in two gradient when a far easier natural route exists a few hundred yards away. When viewed from the flat plateau across the beck to the south, the route just described would appear to be the logical one, but who knows what the road-builders had in mind when they made their choice?

On reaching the level ground, cross through the thick bracken to a gate in the dry-stone wall. Here a track leads to a flat wooden bridge over Ardale Beck, the first drinkable water since leaving Rowgill Burn five miles back along the route. An earth track leads up out of the wide gully onto the moorland plateau; head to the right of a spur of higher ground where the track becomes more clear and where a construction in the hillside is marked on the map as a spring. Looking back, one can imagine the thoughts of those early travellers approaching the high mountain barrier – perhaps a pack train returning north after delivering its consignment of lead ingots to the fort at Brough which, from the quantity of package seals found there, acted as a depot for goods and materials heading for the forts and settlements of the south.

The now clear track leads through a gate and drops down the hill, the rough moorland giving way to the lush pastures of the Eden Valley. A solitary tree marks the entrance to a rough, walled lane which drops down to Bank Hall Farm.

Map 49

The Roman road apparently cuts through where the farm buildings now stand, and the line of the road continues across the fields south to the tiny hamlet of Kirkland by way of the church, but there is no physical evidence to be seen as it crosses the cultivated land.

There was in the past a public footpath which closely followed the Roman route through the fields to Kirkland,

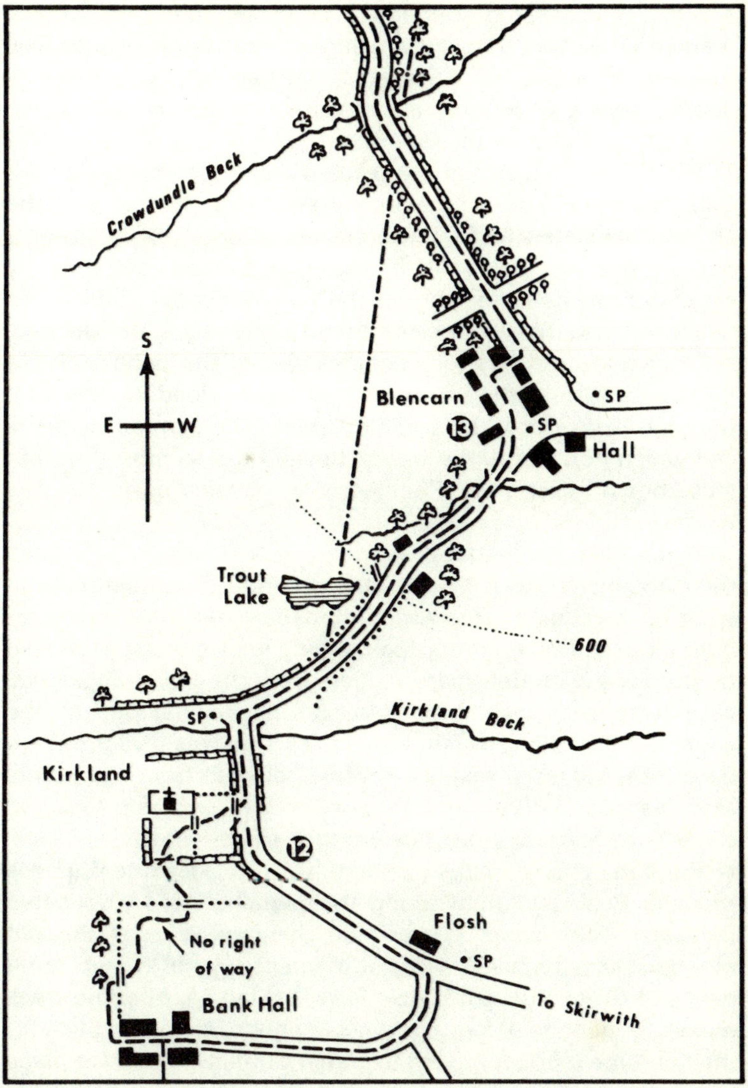
Crowdundle Beck
S
E
W
Blencarn
SP
SP
13
Hall
Trout
Lake
600
Kirkland Beck
SP
Kirkland
12
Flosh
SP
No right
of way
To Skirwith
Bank Hall

Map 49

entering the church grounds by a stone stile, but although still marked on certain maps, it appears to have fallen into disuse. Polite enquiries at the farmhouse may very well prove helpful and so save a three-quarters of a mile detour by way of the farm road as shown on the guide.

Of Kirkland (the name meaning 'land belonging to the Church') there is very little to say and much less to see, the church, dedicated to St Lawrence the Martyr, being its only notable feature. The bells in the twin bellcote are rung by means of chains in the porch, and an old slender stone cross bears witness to its ancient foundations. East of Kirkland, another old route has for centuries served the people of this far-flung parish and is known as the Corpse Road. It climbs up the high slopes of Kirkland Fell beneath the summit of Cross Fell which dominates the valley. Beyond the summit a further well-known route, the Pennine Way, heads north for the border.

Half a mile south-east of Kirkland, near Rambeck, are found the Hanging Walls of Mark Anthony, a sad disappointment in spite of their impressive-sounding name. The three five-foot-high terraces (for such are the hanging walls), were so named by the early Victorian map-markers from the Royal Engineers, who were responsible for this first detailed survey of the county. It is thought by some that the name was given to them by a local wit as a joke on these foreigners from the south. Man-made or natural, their purpose is unknown, and for what there is to see, they are not worth a visit.

From the church, usually open to visitors, our route is across Kirkland Beck and right along the metalled lane signposted Blencarn. The aspect is open as the lane crosses the flat moorland, the high spine of the Pennines, with its two great peaks of Great Dun and Cross Fells, behind us. The fine track makes for good walking, and we can now stride out in style for the first time without having to watch carefully where we place our feet. Patches of harebells and flax mingle with the tall grasses which line the lane. The lane heads south-west to Blencarn and then turns south-east, executing two sides of a rough square. The Roman route heads south from Kirkland across a complicated series of fields, which makes it impractical to try to follow. Shortly before reaching the village of Blencarn, we pass close by a small man-made trout lake. Permits to fish there are obtainable from Blencarn Hall, at the western end of the village.

The lane drops down through a wooded area by a small beck: note the fine stone barn on the left. It crosses the beck and rises to enter the village, which is built around a long, open green, the grass kept trim by a number of brown-and-white goats staked out at intervals. A large house at the southern entrance to the village, named Kirk House, provides accommodation and also doubles as the post office. Pass through the village with its many attractive red and natural sandstone patterned buildings, turning left by Kirk House and now heading south-east along a narrow, enclosed lane. The quiet, almost traffic-free lane makes for pleasant walking as it twists and turns along the contour of the hillside, the ground to the west sloping gently down into the Eden Valley with its rich pastures. Where the lane crossed Crowdundle Beck, the Roman route also crosses heading due south.

Map 50

Two miles to the west, besides the Crowdundle, lie the ancient quarries from which stone was cut to rebuild the fort at Kirkby Thore, and it was here that the two centurions previously mentioned roughly carved their names on the quarry wall. A few hundred yards further along the route, the lane passes the drives to two farms, Lounthwaite on the left and Underwood on the right, the latter being built on the line of the old Roman route. From the farm buildings it is possible to continue the Roman alignment down a private road to where it rejoins the main lane near Gillfoot Bridge, but permission must be obtained before using this alternative route.

Our way is to continue along the main lane, to arrive shortly at a lane leading off to the left and signposted to Milburn. The route is to the right but it is well worth the short diversion to

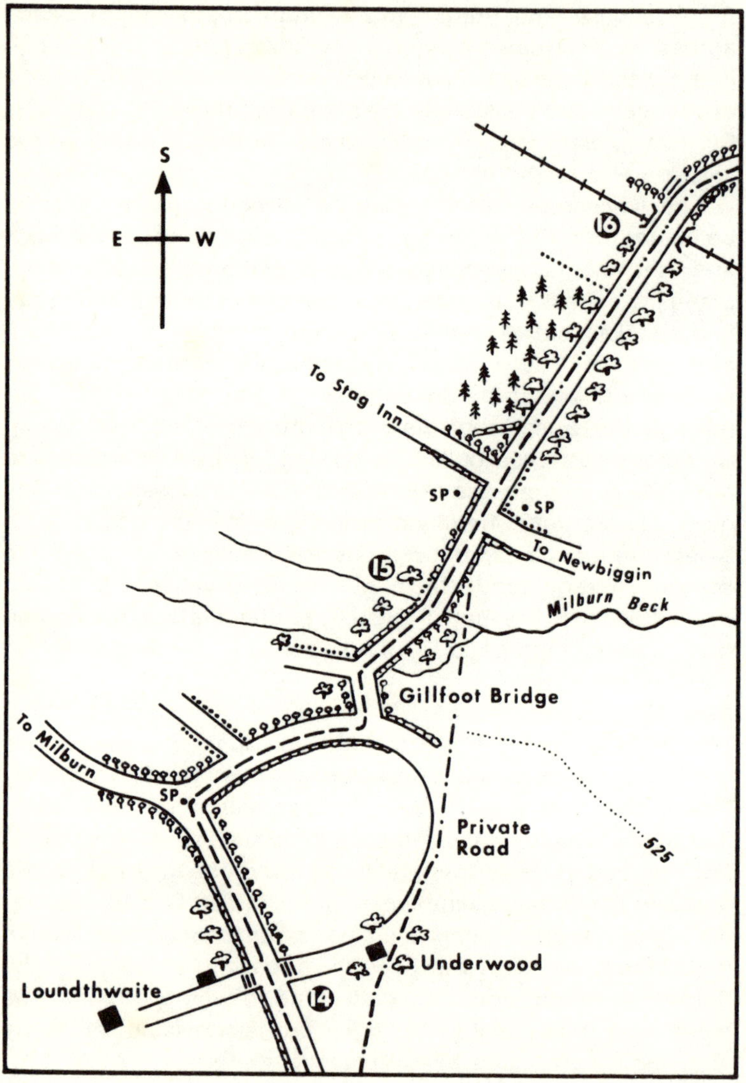
S
E
W
16
To Stag Inn
SP
SP
To Newbiggin
15
Milburn Beck
Gillfoot Bridge
To Milburn
SP
Private Road
525
Underwood
Loundthwaite
14

Map 50

visit this rather unusual village which has, to a great degree, retained its original twelfth-century form. All the houses were built facing inwards round a rectangular village green with only two narrow entrances, which could be walled up in winter or when danger threatened, for in those days there was always a danger of Scottish raids. Behind the houses runs an outer lane into which the cattle where herded from the surrounding fells and from there through narrow, easily defended gaps between the houses and onto the green which could hold a thousand head of cattle and sheep. Today the green's main feature is a tall maypole replaced in 1953 for the Coronation of Elizabeth II. The post office and village store is to the left of the village, but unfortunately there is no pub. The Stag Inn lies only half a mile away at Gullon Holme, but it is off our route, and it would all depend on one's need for a well-earned pint and, of course, on the time of day whether you feel that it is worth the diversion.

Rejoin the route where you turned off to visit Milburn, and continue along it, ignoring the narrow lane on the left. The lane, now called Mill Lane, turns left where the private road from Underwood Farm rejoins it and drops down to cross Kirkhouse Gill by Gillfoot Bridge. Our way then crosses Milburn Beck. The Mill, now disused, is further downstream. We are once more in a direct line with the original Roman road, fragments of which were found when the modern road was being constructed some years ago. As the lane rises gently up the slopes of a low hill, we pass the road to Newbiggin and Temple Sowerby on the right. The latter was named after the Knights Templar who owned property here until the Order was banned in England by Edward II, although reluctantly, after much pressure from the Pope and Philippe IV of France. The property was transferred to the Knights Hospitaller in 1323 and is now known as Acorn House. It belongs to the National Trust. Immediately after passing the Newbiggin road, a further road drops down on the left: this is a possible diversion to visit the Stag Inn, which, as a free house, serves a variety of liquid refreshments plus bar snacks and also has the added facility of a restaurant.

As the lane crosses the flat top of Hale Hill, rolling slopes of rich pastures are revealed. Soon the lane becomes more enclosed as a plantation of conifers joins it on the left, and both sides of the lane support a mixture of broad-leafed trees, where the branches often meet overhead, providing welcome shade on a hot summer day. Elder, oak, sycamore, hawthorn and willow are but a few of the many species, interspersed with wild dog-rose and honeysuckle. After crossing the bridge over the railway line, the long straight lane begins to descend. Just beyond the bridge a glance to the left will reveal the partially hidden bulk of the plaster works where gypsum is mined for the manufacture of plasterboard and other associated products, an industry which provides employment for many of the inhabitants of Kirkby Thore.

Map 51

At the base of the hill the lane turns to pass between the buildings of Hale Grange, one of many sheep granges that once belonged to the great abbeys of the north, whose lands and influence once stretched from deep into Yorkshire to the Cumbrian coast. Immediately through the farm a narrow lane leads off to the left by the side of a large barn: look out for a gate on your right, and pass through it into a small field. Keeping the boundary hedge on your left, cross this field to a broken gate in a wire fence; climbing over the gate, maintain the same direction, with a dry-stone wall on your left to a further poor gate and another climb to follow a faint track with the boundary hedge now on your right, which gives access by gate to a metalled road. This direct route to Hale Grange is marked on the Ordnance Survey map as a public footpath, but it would appear that it has not been in use for some time. For those who do not wish to have to climb over gates, the alternative is to keep straight on after passing the farm, turning left on reaching the main road to rejoin the route where the footpath ends.

The route now follows the road into the village of Kirkby Thore, passing first the village school, still thankfully alive with the happy sound of children, and on the left the parish church

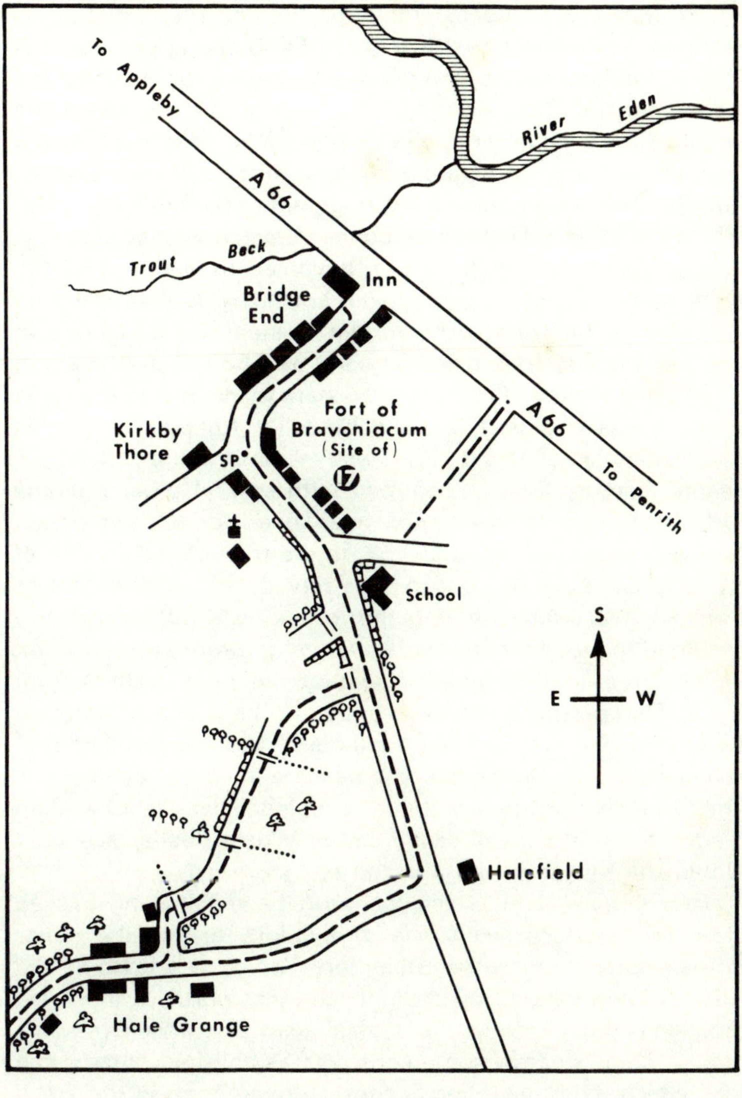
To Appleby
A 66
River Eden
Trout Beck
Inn
Bridge End
Kirkby Thore
SP
Fort of Bravoniacum (Site of)
17
A 66
To Penrith
School
S
E
W
Halefield
Hale Grange

Map 51

of St Michael. A considerable portion of the structure is Norman; its bell was cast in York in 1450 and is probably the largest in Cumbria. Turn right at the crossroads, passing the village general store. As the road curves up the rise, there is a small housing estate on the left, opposite an open field. By the footpath outside the estate is a stone mock-archway, and set into the centre is an old carved fragment of the head of a pillar which could very likely have come from the Roman site.

The site of the Roman fort of Bravoniacum has been for the most part covered by the village, and there is practically no evidence to be seen of its former existence. Excavations of parts of the site took place as early as 1684–7 and again in 1739, when many important finds were made. It is agreed that the fort was originally founded by Julius Agricola during his early campaign of AD 79–80. It was rebuilt in stone early in the second century, and in common with several other Pennine forts it appears to have been abandoned for a short period between about AD 140 and 158. In the third century a unit of Syrian archers are thought to have served here, evidence taken from an altar stone bearing the letters 'N.M.S.S.' which are assumed to stand for *Numerus militum Syrorum sagittariorum*, loosely translated 'a military unit of mounted archers from Syria'. One person by name is known to have served here: an ex-centurion, one P. Licinius Agathopus, who was recalled from retirement in the third century to become the prefect of cavalry. The fort is thought to have been occupied as late as AD 400. In medieval times a small castle, called Whelp Castle, was built within the fort area, but this too has vanished.

The Roman route which we have been following passed close by the north-west side of the fort, to join the major Roman route through the Stainmore Gap, now known as the A66. A short stretch of straight lane just north of the main junction is thought to be the original point where the two roads met. A large veteran settlement was established outside the fort, which must have had a considerable effect on the small local population, leading to a gradual breakdown of hostilities and the establishment of a small town made up of local traders and retired soldiers of all creeds.

There is nothing of particular interest in Kirkby Thore, apart from the Norman church and the village store which we passed along the route. The post office stands back along the main street, and the Bridge End Inn lies by the junction with the A66. The inn serves excellent meals at lunchtime and in the evening but cannot offer any accommodation, although the landlord may be able to advise you as to the nearest available. Appleby, with ample facilities, is only five miles to the south-east, and Penrith eight miles to the north-west; both can be reached by bus.

CHAPTER 7

Brougham Castle (Brocavum) to Brough (Verterae). Margary's route 82. And Brough to Bowes (Lavatrae). Margary's route 82. 40 miles in all.

About the road

The road we are to follow, due west along the northern slopes of the Eden Valley and up across Stainmoor, is one of the oldest Roman campaign routes in the north of England. Although the actual constructed road was probably built by the legions of Agricola during the great advance of AD 79–80, there is strong evidence to show that the route was the one previously used by Cerialis in his earlier campaign of AD 72–3. A series of pre-Agricolan marching camps have been found along the route, spaced one day's march apart, indicating a legionary advance towards Carlisle. Agricola in his turn constructed the road to link his two forces across the northern Pennines with Brougham Castle in the west and Scotch Corner in the east. The forts at Kirkby Thorne, Brough and Bowes were built around the same period to control the area. The route is a natural highway through the high ridges and was, without a doubt, widely used long before the Roman occupation. The importance of this highway through the ages is reflected in the number of medieval castles and keeps which abound along it, a reminder of its turbulent and bloody history.

The route today is still far from peaceful, as it remains the main east-west link and now with considerable extensive 'improvements' is the A66 trunk road, carrying a great volume of private and commercial traffic. Road-widening, which in places has obliterated the road verges, and new dual carriageways have unfortunately made this historic route most unpleasant and, in parts, positively dangerous to walk.

I propose therefore to describe the many points of interest along it and suggest that they be visited by car, a journey which can be safely accomplished in the course of one day.

The Route

Leave the site of the fort at Brougham Castle by the minor road B6262, heading north-east, which very soon joins the A66(T), the course of the Roman road between Carlisle and Scotch Corner. Shortly after joining the main road we pass on the right a tall stone pillar known as the Countess Pillar, a monument set up by Lady Anne Clifford in memory of her mother, who died in a coach at this spot 'on ye third of April 1616'. Several Roman tombstones were found alongside the road not far from here, a common Roman practice. Our next point of interest is approximately six miles ahead, half a mile beyond Temple Sowerby, which was mentioned in the previous chapter. Look out for a lay-by on the left-hand side of the road. Here, looking very sad and sorry for itself within an iron cage, are the remains of a Roman milestone, one of only two milestones in the whole of Britain which still stand in the original position as placed by the Romans. There is nothing to identify the stone as it stands neglected in the hedgerow surrounded by litter, and I received some funny looks as I took a photograph of it.

A further mile east we pass Kirkby Thore and the site of the Roman fort of Bravoniacum, again mentioned in the previous chapter. Should it be lunchtime, I can recommend the Bridge End Inn at the main road end of the village.

Our next port of call is the ancient county town of Appleby roughly seven miles ahead. The new dual carriageway now bypasses Appleby. Turn off to Appleby where indicated and, as the slip road turns left again, take note of a narrow lane which continues parallel with the new road in an easterly direction. This is a short stretch of the original Roman route.

Apart from the Roman road, known as High Street, passing nearby, the town is not known to have any Roman connections, but it is well worth a visit if time is not too pressing. Founded in early Norman times with the building of a keep, it has had a turbulent history. Sacked by the Scots, decimated by the Black Death and bombarded during the Civil Wars, when the Loyalist levies took refuge in the castle, it is today a quiet town basking in the reflected glory of the past.

In 1970 the last Assize Court was held, and in 1974, following the Local Government Act of 1972, the town ceased to be a Borough and County Town, the old counties of Westmorland and Cumberland being combined to form the new County of Cumbria. In 1976, however, true to the old stubborn northern spirit, the town was renamed 'Appleby in Westmorland'. The small town has nine pubs and several restaurants and cafés catering for the passing visitor.

The castle was restored by Lady Anne Clifford in the seventeenth century and is now in the hands of a public company. Admission to the castle and the extensive grounds, where a large collection of rare animals and birds is well displayed, is through the gatehouse at the top of the main street. An interesting group of buildings on the left-hand side of this lime-tree-lined avenue are almshouses founded by the Lady Anne in 1651. Her body now lies enshrined in a black marble tomb in the parish church. This redoubtable lady, on the opening of her tomb, was found to be under five feet tall.

One of the most notable events in Appleby takes place in early June, when the six-centuries-old Appleby Horse Fair takes place. Thousands of gypsies, tinkers and horse-dealers gather on the fell above the town showing off their horses and foals. So numerous are the crowds that the fair spills over into the town. Wild-looking gypsy men gallop madly up and down the main road riding bare-backed on equally wild-looking ponies – some of the hotels and pubs close their doors. Not the ideal time to visit Appleby but none the less an interesting experience.

Leave Appleby by the B542 road in a south-easterly direction. To the left, where it joins the A66, is the site of a large Iron Age earthworks, no doubt abandoned when the legions marched this way. Between here and the castle and Roman site at Brough, there is much evidence of the present-day military presence in the area. Along the ridges to the north red flags fly, warnings that the army's artillery firing-ranges are in operation. Helicopters appear from time to time hovering above the tree tops; occasionally a convoy of military hardware will rumble past. I was in the snug of a local inn when a troop of armoured cars drew into the car-park and the pub wag remarked that we could sleep easy tonight, the Scots wouldn't get far across the border. Memories are long here in the north, and it *was* Glasgow Holiday Week.

As we approach Brough, turn off the A66 which now bypasses the village, much to the relief of its inhabitants, and turn right by the Golden Fleece Inn, one of many pubs, onto the A685 Kirkby Stephen road. The second turn right leads to the small hamlet of Church Brough and the site of the Roman fort of Verterae.

The castle stands on a section of the Roman site in an elevated position overlooking Swindale Beck. It was originally Norman and dates from about 1092, but much of what remains is the result of the rebuilding which took place after its demolition by the Scots under William the Lion. It fell into disrepair again by 1245, and there is evidence to show that it was rebuilt again in the late thirteenth and fourteenth centuries. In 1659–62 Lady Anne Clifford restored it, together with the castles of Brougham and Skipton. The castle is now in the charge of the Department of the Environment who care for the site and charge a small fee for admission. A full description and history of the castle can be obtained from the custodian.

The Roman earthworks are well preserved but no Roman masonry is now visible. From the large number of lead dispatch seals found on the site and the fact that a unit of the Numerus Directorum was stationed here, experts believe that the fort acted as a forwarding depot for packages and consignments routed south from the northern forts. A dedication slab dated AD 197, now almost illegible, is to be found in the nearby church porch. Climb to the top of the keep (a new flight of stairs has been constructed), and try to imagine the view in Roman times, the Roman sentry gazing east towards the line of signal towers which carried messages over the bleak Stainmore Fells. The fort is thought to have been occupied until the final days of Roman control, and the *VII Cohors Thracus eq*, a cavalry unit originally recruited in Bulgaria, was stationed here in the third century.

Four and a half miles after re-joining the A66, the road once again becomes a dual carriageway. A hundred yards beyond this point a roadway signpost indicates a minor road to the right, leading to South Stainmore, Barras and Kaber. Turn off the road here to a clear parking space besides the signpost on the left-hand carriageway. A pathway sign points to a clear, broad path heading up the fellside and is reached through a gate in the boundary wall. The broad path, named on the sign as the Maiden Way, must not be confused with the other Maiden Way heading north from Kirkby Thore. After a short way the grass-covered path turns off to the right, leaving the dry-stone wall to continue up the fellside, on a well-defined wide agger. The remains of the Roman fortlet is on the right of the causeway.

Now named Maiden Castle, it was a small post probably holding about fifty men and was a link in the signalling system between Brough and Bowes. The remains consist of four sides of stony banks about six feet high representing the original stone defences, and there is a double ditch on the north side indicated by reeds. It is thought to date from the second century, which probably also dates the other signal stations on the Stainmore route. The position commands a magnificent view over the Eden Valley, and in good visibility the fort site at Brough can be identified by the castle in the middle distance. To the east, the signal station on a small hill called Roper Castle, south of the road, was a vital link in the system

Map 52

Two miles from Maiden Castle, east along the A66, we shall find the finest and best-preserved marching camp in Britain.

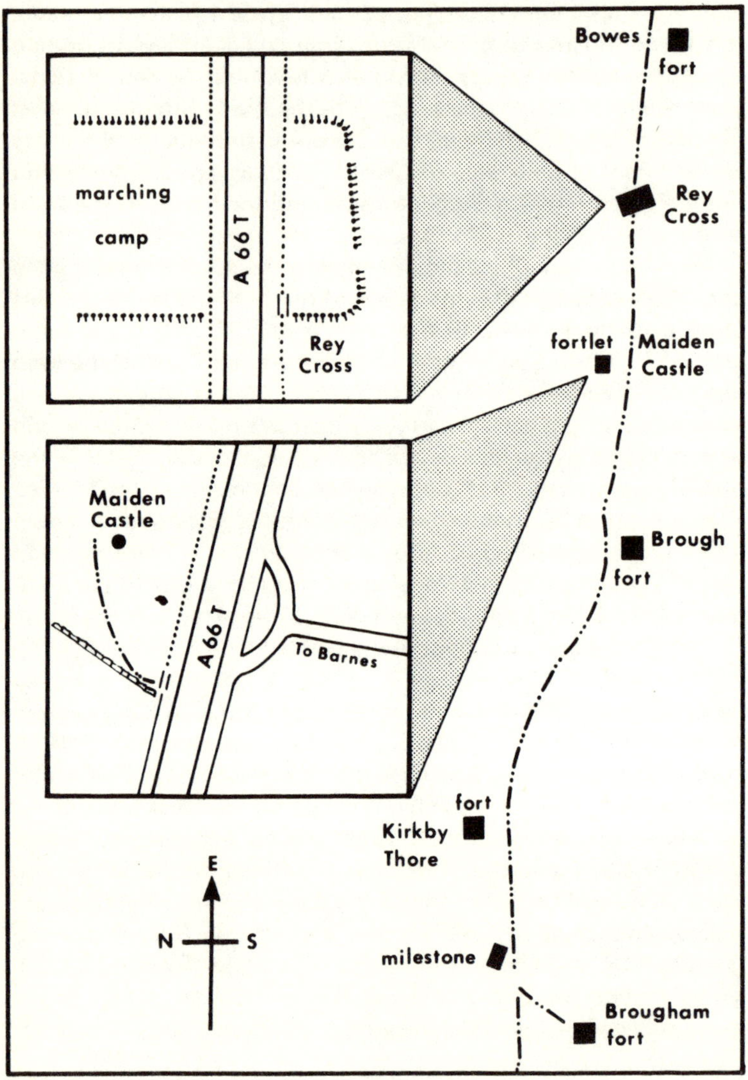
Bowes
fort
marching
camp
A 66 T
Rey
Cross
Rey
Cross
fortlet
Maiden
Castle
Maiden
Castle
A 66 T
To Barnes
Brough
fort
fort
Kirkby
Thore
E
N
S
milestone
Brougham
fort

Map 52

Look out for a rough lay-by on the south side of the road soon after crossing the border into the county of Durham: here you will find the Rey Cross, or what remains of it, surrounded by a low iron rail. Walk forward to the parking sign where a broken gate leads onto the open moor, cross the gate and head due south across the rough ground to where it falls steeply down a ravine; here turn to view the southern ramparts of this magnificent earthworks. Quarrying has removed part of the western side, and some of the northern ramparts have sunk into the boggy ground, but elsewhere it is traceable by the sheer bulk of its ramparts, twenty feet wide and often over six feet high. There were eleven gateways, nine of which have survived, each protected by a forward mound called a *titula*. The camp at Rey Cross (its Roman name, if it ever had one, is not known) was large enough to hold a legion of 5,500 men and probably held the tents of the Ninth Legion under Petillius Cerialis during his campaign against the Brigantes in AD 72–3. The road passes through the southern section of the camp, the main part being on the north side of the road which was originally built to pass through two gates of the camp.

Due south and four miles away can just be seen, on the high ridge, the Tan Hill Inn, the highest pub in England and a welcome resting place for weary walkers of the Pennine Way. Our way is still east, where, after approximately two miles, we pass the Bowes Moor Hotel: a few hundred yards beyond the hotel pull in onto a lay-by on the right. Cross the road near the parking sign, and the Roman signal station is twenty-five yards north of the wire fence. The remains consist of a ditch and circular rampart; the best-preserved side is to the north. The signal tower would have been inside the enclosure and constructed of timber. This would have been one of several signal towers relaying messages between the forts. The one to the west can just be spotted in clear weather about three miles away and a mile south of the road, at what is called Roper Castle. To the east a spur of land blocks the view to the fort at Bowes, and another signal station was needed, but there is now no trace on the ground.

A further two miles east lies the village of Bowes, and again the new road by-passes it. The castle and Roman site lie in the centre of the village, to the left of the main street, behind the church – in fact the church and cemetary lie on part of the fort site. The Norman keep is open to the public, and no charge is made. It lies within the north-west angle of the fort of Lavatrae, and the church occupies the north-east corner. Excavations in 1966–7 revealed that the original ramparts were raised by Agricola about AD 78 and consist of large river boulders set in clay. In the second century part of the ramparts was cut back to receive a stone wall which was later replaced by a second wall, eight feet thick. An inscription, now at Cambridge, records that the fort was 'burnt by the violence of fire' and was restored in the governorship of Virius Lupus (AD 197–202). The fort was then garrisoned by a unit of the *Ala Hispanorum Vettonum C*, a cavalry squadron recruited in Spain. Later, in 208, this was replaced by the *I Cohors Thracum eq*, another cavalry unit recruited, in the first instance, in Bulgaria. A dedication slab to the Emperor Severus and his sons is in the north transept of the church but is nearly illegible.

Bowes today is a quiet place compared with former days when the A66 passed through its centre. The Ancient Unicorn Inn provides refreshments for the rare visitor.

It is here at Bowes that we must finish our journey, for already we are well over the border. The Roman road continued, of course, one route heading north-east to the fort at Binchester, the other south-west to meet the great north-eastern route from the legionary fortress at York.

I can only hope that this account and guide of some of the Roman roads of Cumbria will have helped to fire the imagination and to foster an appreciation of this important period of British history: over four hundred years of comparative stability, probably the longest this country will ever know, when Britain was not just a province of Rome but an important and valued member of the Empire, and when a man could travel from Carlisle to Jerusalem without passport or visa.

NOTES

NOTES

Note 1: The Roman Mile

Many profound articles have been written on the subject of the Roman mile and its estimated length in modern terms. There have been as many as twelve estimates, ranging from 1,600 to 1,831 yards. All the experts seem to agree that the Roman mile was made up of a thousand double paces of five feet, so that it would appear that it is the length of the double pace that is in question. A thousand paces of an imperial five feet works out at 1,666 yards as against the present mile of 1,760 yards, but based on remaining records it has been generally accepted that the measurement of 1,680 yards is nearer to the true figure. The Roman foot (*pes*) is equivalent to 0.926 feet imperial measure, and this would give us the lowest estimate, slightly over 1,660 yards. With the aid of a calculator I worked out the required length of double pace to match all the various estimates and found that there was only an eight-inch variance between the highest and the lowest. It has been suggested that the Roman mile became shorter when the route crossed through hilly country, and this is perfectly feasible. As every walker knows, the pace shortens as the gradient increases. Which brings us to the question: how did the Romans measure their miles? Did they use some sort of measuring rod or did they simply count a thousand paces as they marched along? I think the latter is more likely, and it would certainly account for the many discrepancies.

I have tested the feasibility of the Roman marching pace over several stretches of the original routes. Walking at the

British Army's regulation pace of 120 paces to the minute, i.e. sixty double paces, I was able to cover a distance of 1,650 yards in fifteen minutes, marching nine hundred double paces. This equates well with the Roman measurement and a pace of twenty miles in five hours.

The minimum height of the legionary was five feet seven inches, which makes a five-foot double pace quite reasonable. It is an interesting fact that the pacing sticks carried by drill sergeants of the Brigade of Guards measure a double pace of exactly five feet.

The distances quoted in the guide are in modern miles, for the difference under ten miles is not worth considering, and even at twenty miles it is only about one mile. I suppose to keep up to date I should 'go metric' but that really would not be in keeping with the spirit of the book. Readers with metric maps will have to convert.

Note 2: The Legions of the Roman Empire

The Legions, of which there were usually twenty-eight, held pride of place in the Roman army. With an establishment of approximately 5,500 men each, this gave a total legionary strength of about 160,000 men, fifty per cent of the armed forces of Rome. The Legions were distributed mainly along or near the frontiers, with four in Britain, although later this was reduced to three. Although recruitment to the Roman army was theoretically based on conscription, there seems to have been little difficulty in filling the ranks with volunteers.

The volunteer had to appear before a board of officers for selection. Although the minimum height requirement was five feet seven a height of five feet ten was considered more desirable. He underwent a stringent medical examination, and his character would also be closely scrutinized. Once accepted for service, the recruit swore an oath of allegiance to the Emperor and was posted to a training camp, several of which have been identified in Britain. All legionaries had to be full citizens of Rome, but this did not mean that they were all men of Italian origin. On completing twenty-five years' service, the legionary was given the choice of a land grant or a sum of money and officially was then allowed to marry (this ruling was dropped in the second century). Most veterans settled in the country in which they had served. For further and deeper study, consult the Bibliography.

The legion of the first century AD consisted of ten cohorts of heavily armed infantry. Cohorts 2–10 were made up of six 'centuries' of about eighty men, each century commanded by a centurion. The first cohort comprised five centuries, each of 160 men. The centurion who commanded the first century of the first cohort was also the chief centurion of the legion – the ambition of every new recruit. The chief centurion held his position for one year only and quite frequently passed on to a higher position, e.g. a camp commander or command of an auxiliary legion. If in battle a legionary commander were killed or badly wounded, the chief centurion would often take over command of the legion, being the most experienced officer present. Attached to the legion were 120 horsemen who acted as scouts and dispatch riders.

Note 3: Marching Camps

When engaged on a campaign or any other occasion when a legion or part of a legion was in the field, at the end of the day's march a fortified camp was constructed. Four flags would be placed to mark the corners of the chosen site and a ditch dug surrounding the camp area; this would be approximately a yard wide and deep. The earth and turf from the ditch were used to build a rampart into which was set a close fence of wooden stakes about five feet in length, each man carrying two of these as part of his equipment; the stakes were then lashed together to form a palisade. The size and construction of these 'marching camps' was strictly laid down in manuals, the size determined by a formula depending on the number of men, and the shape, although sometimes varied to suit the terrain, usually rectangular with rounded corners. Within the entrenched area the camp was formed, and since the layout of every camp was always the same, each unit knew exactly where to pitch its tents. The tents, not unlike the modern ridge-tent in appearance, were made up of squares of goat-hide and housed eight men. The following day the camp would be dismantled and the earthwork levelled before the legion marched on.

Traces of several of these camps have been found, notably over Stainmore along a route towards Carlisle, and a fine example in the heart of the Yorkshire Dales.

Note 4: Identification of Alone

A valuable guide to the identification of Roman place-names in Britain is the *Antonine Itinerary*, which was prepared for the information of official travellers, giving place-names and staging points in distances along the major roads throughout the Empire. The work appears to date from the second century. The *Inter Britanniarum* relates to the roads of Britain and is divided into fifteen 'seconds', the first giving the total distance from terminus to terminus and then the individual mileage between each staging point. The section in which we are interested is the Tenth Inter, Ravenglass (Glannaventa) to Chesterton, Staffs (Medidano), a distance of 150 miles. Coming north, Ribchester is definitely identified as Bremetennacum, to be followed by Galacum, the fort at Overborough, a distance of twenty-seven Roman miles. The next station quoted is that of Alone, nineteen miles, and then Galava at Ambleside twelve miles, and a further eighteen miles to Glannaventa.

It is possible that Alone may be identified as the fort at Low Borrow Bridge, situated at the junction of Borrow Beck and the River Lune, or Lon to give it its older name, a possible survival of the Roman name, Galacum, nineteen Roman miles south is also situated at a similar junction of the Lune and the Leck, previously known as the Lac. The name 'Galacum' has in fact been interpreted to mean 'noisy stream', a direct reference to Leck Beck.

The identification of Low Borrow Bridge as Alone does deserve serious consideration but also opens up a further interesting speculation. According to the *Itinerary*, the next staging point from Alone was Galava at Ambleside, with a distance of twelve miles, which leads to the possibility of a hitherto unknown high-level route across the fells.

Note 5: Auxiliary Legions

The auxiliaries were recruited from amongst the warlike frontier tribes of the Empire. They were originally formed to serve in the area of their homeland and were often commanded by local chieftains, but in the first century a policy change decreed that units be sent to serve in provinces far away from their own lands. They were formed into cohorts of five hundred men which were commanded by a Roman officer. Later larger units were formed approximately a thousand strong. Weapons of the auxiliary infantry were usually a sword and short spear, but some units specialized in special skills, such as the Cretan archers and Balearic slingers. Although some auxiliaries wore no armour, those who did wore either mail or scale armour, and their helmets were a cheaper version of the current legionary type. Naturally enough, the legionaries regarded the non-citizen troops as inferiors, but it was the auxiliaries who really manned the frontiers of the fighting. It became the policy of Roman commanders to place the auxiliaries in the forefront of the battle and hold the legions in reserve, thus saving 'Roman' manpower.

After serving twenty-five years the auxiliary was granted Roman citizenship, as were his children. As generations came and went, the sons of these veterans, now Roman citizens, joined the same local units in which their fathers had served, and the rigid class distinction between the legions and the *auxilia* began to fade, finally to disappear in the third century. Their contribution to the establishment of the Roman world has been badly under-estimated in favour of the more glamorous image of the legions.

Note 6: The Legionary's Burden

The weight carried by the Roman legionary has been debated, and many doubt the possibility of such burdens being carried over long distances and over rough terrain. But it must be remembered that these men were the elite of the Roman army, chosen for their physical fitness and stature. They were given extensive training, a large part being devoted to route marching in full equipment. For a modern equivalent it was reported in a newspaper that a Commando Brigade on exercise recently marched thirty miles in six hours carrying eighty-pound packs. Whilst in Burma in 1944 the Chindits, from brigadier to private, carried seventy pounds on their backs plus fifty pounds of equipment and weapons and another eighteen pounds of rations. This monstrous load was carried across some of the worst terrain in the world, through monsoons, for the whole of the campaign.

BIBLIOGRAPHY

BIBLIOGRAPHY

The Ordnance Survey Map of Roman Britain
The Roman Roads of Britain, Ivan D. Margary
Britannia, a History of Roman Britain, Sheppard Frere
Roman Britain, Peter Salway
Roman Britain, John Wacher
Exploring Roman Britain, P.J. Helm
A Guide to Roman Remains in Britain, Roger J.A. Wilson
Romans in Britain, Rodney Legg
The People of Roman Britain, Anthony Birley
Romans in the North West, T.W. Potter
Roman Britain from the Air, S.S. Frere and J.K.S. St Joseph
Roman Inscriptions in Britain, R.G. Collingwood and R.P. Wright
Wanderings in Roman Britain, Arthur Weigall
Roman Eskdale, Tom Garlick
The Roman Army, Peter Connoly
The Roman Soldier, G.R. Watson
The Roman Army of Britain, P.A. Holder
The Armour of the Roman Legions, Russel Robinson
Roman Civilisation, Lewis and Reinhold
A Guide to Prehistoric England, Nicholas Thomas
The Environment of Early Man in Britain, John G. Evans
Signposts of the Past, Margaret Gelling
Celtic Britain, Lloyd Laing
The Ancient Bridges of the North of England, E. Jervoise
Forgotten Railways of North West England, John Marshall
British Native Ponies and English Breeds, Charles Stratton
A History of British Trees, Gerald Wilkinson

The Naturalised Animals of the British Isles, Christopher Dever
A History of Cumberland and Westmorland, William Rollingson
Cumbria, A Guide to the Lake District and its County, John Parker
A Pictorial Guide to the Lakeland Fells, A. Wainwright
Still the Real Lakeland, A.H. Griffin
Cumbrian Villages, Kenneth Smith
A Portrait of the Howgills and Upper Eden Valley, Michael Ffinch
The Countrygoers North, Jessica Lofthouse
Lancashire–Westmorland Highway, Jessica Lofthouse

INDEX

Index